The Yale Shakespeare.

◄◄◄◄◄◄◄◄◄◄◄◄◄◄◄◄◄◄◄◄►►►►►►►►►►►►►►►►►►►

HAMLET

NEW EDITION REVISED BY

TUCKER BROOKE

PUBLISHED ON THE FUND
GIVEN TO THE YALE UNIVERSITY PRESS IN 1917
BY THE MEMBERS OF THE
KINGSLEY TRUST ASSOCIATION
(SCROLL AND KEY SOCIETY OF YALE COLLEGE)
TO COMMEMORATE THE SEVENTY-FIFTH ANNIVERSARY
OF THE FOUNDING OF THE SOCIETY

This new edition of Hamlet and a number of other plays in THE YALE SHAKESPEARE has been prepared by TUCKER BROOKE who has used, added to, and brought up to date the work of the previous editors whose names appear with his in the separate volumes.

The Tragedy of Hamlet Prince of Denmark

EDITED BY TUCKER BROOKE

AND

JACK RANDALL CRAWFORD

New Haven · Yale University Press

LONDON · GEOFFREY CUMBERLEGE

OXFORD UNIVERSITY PRESS

CONTENTS

The facsimile opposite represents the title-page of the Elizabethan Club copy of the Second Quarto (1604), the best text of the play. Three copies bearing this date and three others bearing the date 1605 are known to survive.

THE
Tragicall Historie of
HAMLET,

Prince of Denmarke.

By William Shakespeare.

Newly imprinted and enlarged to almost as much
againe as it was, according to the true and perfect
Coppie.

AT LONDON,
Printed by I. R. for N. L. and are to be sold at his
shoppe vnder Saint Dunstons Church in
Fleetstreet. 1604.

[THE ACTORS' NAMES]

CLAUDIUS, *the new king of Denmark.*

HAMLET, *son to the late, and nephew to the present king.*

FORTINBRAS, *prince of Norway.*

POLONIUS, *a lord and high official (probably Lord Chamberlain).*

LAERTES, *his son.*

HORATIO, *the friend of Hamlet.*

VOLTIMAND
CORNELIUS
ROSENCRANTZ } *courtiers.*
GUILDENSTERN
OSRIC

MARCELLUS, *a Danish officer.*

FRANCISCO
BERNARDO } *soldiers on sentry duty.*

REYNALDO, *servant to Polonius.*

A Norwegian captain.

Players on tour.

Two clowns, gravediggers.

English ambassador, a priest, a gentleman, soldiers, sailor, messenger, and various attendants.

GERTRUDE, *queen of Denmark and mother of Hamlet.*

OPHELIA, *daughter of Polonius.*

GHOST *of Hamlet's father.*

SCENE: *the royal castle of Elsinore (Helsingør), Denmark, and its environs.]*

The Actors' Names; *cf. n.*

The Tragedy of Hamlet, Prince of Denmark

ACT FIRST

SCENE FIRST.

[Elsinore. Platform of the Castle]

Enter Bernardo and Francisco, two Sentinels.

Ber. Who's there?
Fran. Nay, answer me; stand, and unfold yourself.
Ber. Long live the king!
Fran. Bernardo?   4
Ber. He.
Fran. You come most carefully upon your hour.
Ber. 'Tis now struck twelve; get thee to bed, Francisco.
Fran. For this relief much thanks; 'tis bitter cold,   8
And I am sick at heart.
   Ber. Have you had quiet guard?
   Fran.   Not a mouse stirring.
   Ber. Well, good night.
If you do meet Horatio and Marcellus,   12
The rivals of my watch, bid them make haste.

Enter Horatio and Marcellus.

Fran. I think I hear them. Stand, ho! Who is there?
Hor. Friends to this ground.
Mar.   And liegemen to the Dane.

S. d. Platform: *level space on castle ramparts*
3 Long . . . king!; *cf. n.*   13 rivals: *partners*
15 Friends . . . Dane; *cf. n.*

Fran. Give you good night.

Mar.   O, farewell, honest soldier.   16
Who hath reliev'd you?

Fran.   Bernardo hath my place.
Give you good night.   *Exit Francisco.*

Mar.   Holla! Bernardo!

Ber.   Say,—
What, is Horatio there?

Hor.   A piece of him.

Ber. Welcome, Horatio; welcome, good Marcellus.   20

Mar. What, has this thing appear'd again to-night?

Ber. I have seen nothing.

Mar. Horatio says 'tis but our fantasy,
And will not let belief take hold of him   24
Touching this dreaded sight twice seen of us.
Therefore I have entreated him along
With us to watch the minutes of this night,
That if again this apparition come,   28
He may approve our eyes and speak to it.

Hor. Tush, tush! 'twill not appear.

Ber.   Sit down awhile,
And let us once again assail your ears,
That are so fortified against our story,   32
What we have two nights seen.

Hor.   Well, sit we down,
And let us hear Bernardo speak of this.

Ber. Last night of all,
When yond same star that's westward from the pole   36
Had made his course t' illume that part of heaven

16 Give you: *God give you*   19 piece; *cf. n.*
23 fantasy: *imagination*   29 approve: *confirm*
31 assail your ears; *i.e., try to tell you*   37 his; *cf. n.*

Where now it burns, Marcellus and myself,
The bell then beating one,—

Enter Ghost.

   Mar. Peace! break thee off; look, where it comes
      again!   40
   Ber. In the same figure, like the king that's dead.
   Mar. Thou art a scholar; speak to it, Horatio.
   Ber. Looks 'a not like the king? mark it, Horatio.
   Hor. Most like: it harrows me with fear and won-
      der.   44
   Ber. It would be spoke to.
   Mar.   Question it, Horatio.
   Hor. What art thou that usurp'st this time of night,
Together with that fair and warlike form
In which the majesty of buried Denmark   48
Did sometimes march? by heaven I charge thee, speak!
   Mar. It is offended.
   Ber.   See! it stalks away.
   Hor. Stay! speak, speak! I charge thee, speak!

                                Exit Ghost.

   Mar. 'Tis gone, and will not answer.   52
   Ber. How now, Horatio! you tremble and look pale.
Is not this something more than fantasy?
What think you on 't?
   Hor. Before my God, I might not this believe   56
Without the sensible and true avouch
Of mine own eyes.

---

42 scholar; *cf. n.*   43 'a: *dialect form of 'he' (sometimes 'it')*
43 mark: *observe closely*   45 It . . . to; *cf. n.*
49 sometimes: *formerly*
57 sensible: *involving the use of one of the senses*   avouch:
   assurance

Mar.   Is it not like the king?

Hor. As thou art to thyself:

Such was the very armor he had on   60
When he the ambitious Norway combated;
So frown'd he once, when, in an angry parle,
He smote the sleaded pole-axe on the ice.
'Tis strange.   64

Mar. Thus twice before, and jump at this dead hour,
With martial stalk hath he gone by our watch.

Hor. In what particular thought to work I know not;
But in the gross and scope of my opinion,   68
This bodes some strange eruption to our state.

Mar. Good now, sit down, and tell me, he that knows,
Why this same strict and most observant watch
So nightly toils the subject of the land;   72
And why such daily cast of brazen cannon,
And foreign mart for implements of war;
Why such impress of shipwrights, whose sore task
Does not divide the Sunday from the week;   76
What might be toward, that this sweaty haste
Doth make the night joint-laborer with the day:
Who is 't that can inform me?

Hor.   That can I;

At least, the whisper goes so. Our last king,   80
Whose image even but now appear'd to us,

---

62 parle: *verbal encounter*
63 sleaded: *weighted (as a sledge-hammer)*   pole-axe: *battle-ax; cf. n.*
65 jump: *just*   67 thought: *train of thinking*
68 gross and scope: *general drift*   70 Good now; *cf. n.*
72 toils: *causes to toil*   subject: *people, subjects*
73 cast: *founding*   74 mart: *traffic*
75 impress: *enforced service*   77 toward: *in preparation*

Was, as you know, by Fortinbras of Norway,
Thereto prick'd on by a most emulate pride,
Dar'd to the combat; in which our valiant Hamlet   84
(For so this side of our known world esteem'd him,)
Did slay this Fortinbras; who by a seal'd compact,
Well ratified by law and heraldry,
Did forfeit with his life all those his lands   88
Which he stood seiz'd of, to the conqueror;
Against the which a moiety competent
Was gaged by our king, which had return'd
To the inheritance of Fortinbras,   92
Had he been vanquisher; as, by the same cov'nant,
And carriage of the article design'd,
His fell to Hamlet. Now, sir, young Fortinbras,
Of unimproved mettle hot and full,   96
Hath in the skirts of Norway here and there
Shark'd up a list of lawless resolutes,
For food and diet, to some enterprise
That hath a stomach in 't; which is no other,
As it doth well appear unto our state,   101
But to recover of us by strong hand
And terms compulsatory, those foresaid lands

83 prick'd on: *incited*   emulate: *ambitious*
85 this side . . . world; *i.e., all Europe*
87 law and heraldry; *cf. n.*   89 seiz'd of: *possessed of; cf. n.*
90 moiety competent: *equal amount*
91 gaged: *staked*   93 cov'nant; *cf. n.*
94 carriage: *import*   design'd: *drawn up*
96 unimproved mettle: *untested courage*   hot and full: *exceedingly ardent*
97 skirts: *outskirts*
98 Shark'd up: *picked up at haphazard*   list: *cf. n.*   resolutes: *desperadoes*
100 stomach: *cf. n.*
103 compulsatory: *involving compulsion*

So by his father lost. And this, I take it,   104
Is the main motive of our preparations,
The source of this our watch and the chief head
Of this post-haste and romage in the land.

«*Ber.* I think it be no other but e'en so;   108
Well may it sort that this portentous figure
Comes armed through our watch, so like the king
That was and is the question of these wars.

Hor. A mote it is to trouble the mind's eye.   112
In the most high and palmy state of Rome,
A little ere the mightiest Julius fell,
The graves stood tenantless and the sheeted dead
Did squeak and gibber in the Roman streets.   116
[Astounding portents fill'd the element,]
As stars with trains of fire and dews of blood,
Disasters in the sun; and the moist star
Upon whose influence Neptune's empire stands
Was sick almost to doomsday with eclipse;   120
And even the like precurse of fear'd events,
As harbingers preceding still the fates
And prologue to the omen coming on,
Have heaven and earth together demonstrated
Unto our climatures and countrymen.»   125

---

106 head: *origin*   107 romage: *commotion, bustle*
108–125 *Not in Folio*   109 sort: *fit*
112 mote: *minute particle of dust*
113 palmy state: *flourishing sovereignty*
116 Astounding . . . element; *cf. n.*   117 As: *such as*
118 Disasters: *unfavorable omens*   moist star: *moon*
120 sick . . . doomsday; *cf. n.*
121 precurse: *heralding*   fear'd; *cf. n.*
122 still: *constantly*
123 prologue: *introduction*   omen: *catastrophe*
125 climatures; *cf. n.*

Enter Ghost again.

But, soft, behold! lo, where it comes again!
I'll cross it, though it blast me. Stay, illusion!
If thou hast any sound, or use of voice,   128
Speak to me!   *It spreads his arms.*
If there be any good thing to be done,
That may to thee do ease and grace to me,
Speak to me!   132
If thou art privy to thy country's fate,
Which happily foreknowing may avoid,
O speak!
Or if thou hast uphoarded in thy life   136
Extorted treasure in the womb of earth,
For which, they say, you spirits oft walk in death,
                                The cock crows.
Speak of it: stay, and speak! Stop it, Marcellus. 139
    Mar. Shall I strike at it with my partisan?
    Hor. Do, if it will not stand.
    Ber.   'Tis here!
    Hor.   'Tis here!
                            Exit Ghost.

    Mar. 'Tis gone!
We do it wrong, being so majestical,
To offer it the show of violence;   144
For it is, as the air, invulnerable,
And our vain blows malicious mockery.
    Ber. It was about to speak when the cock crew.
    Hor. And then it started like a guilty thing
Upon a fearful summons. I have heard,   149

127 cross: *meet, face*   129 s.d. his: *its (the ghost's)*
131 [do] grace: *do honor to*   134 happily: *haply*
136 uphoarded; *cf. n.*   140 partisan; *cf. n.*

The cock, that is the trumpet to the morn,
Doth with his lofty and shrill-sounding throat
Awake the god of day; and at his warning,   152
Whether in sea or fire, in earth or air,
Th' extravagant and erring spirit hies
To his confine; and of the truth herein
This present object made probation.   156
    Mar. It faded on the crowing of the cock.
Some say that ever 'gainst that season comes
Wherein our Saviour's birth is celebrated,
This bird of dawning singeth all night long   160
And then, they say, no spirit dare stir abroad;
The nights are wholesome; then no planets strike,
No fairy takes, nor witch hath power to charm,
So hallow'd and so gracious is that time.   164
    Hor. So have I heard and do in part believe it.
But, look, the morn in russet mantle clad,
Walks o'er the dew of yon high eastward hill.
Break we our watch up; and by my advice   168
Let us impart what we have seen to-night
Unto young Hamlet, for, upon my life,
This spirit, dumb to us, will speak to him.
Do you consent we shall acquaint him with it,
As needful in our loves, fitting our duty?   173
    Mar. Let's do 't, I pray; and I this morning know
Where we shall find him most conveniently.   *Exeunt.*

150 cock; *cf. n.*
154 extravagant: *vagrant*   erring: *wandering*   hies: *hastens*
155 confine: *place of confinement*   156 probation: *proof*
157–164 Cf. *n.*   158 'gainst that: *by the time that*
162 planets strike: *cf. n.*   163 takes: *bewitches*
164 gracious: *instinct with goodness*
166 russet: *gray or reddish-brown (betokening dull weather)*

SCENE SECOND.

[*The King's Council Chamber*]

Flourish. Enter Claudius King of Denmark, Gertrude the
Queen [members of the] Council as Polonius and
his son Laertes, [Voltimand and Cornelius,] Hamlet,
cum aliis.

speech flowery and artificial

   King. Though yet of Hamlet our dear brother's death
The memory be green, and that it us befitted
To bear our hearts in grief and our whole kingdom
To be contracted in one brow of woe,   4
Yet so far hath discretion fought with nature
That we with wisest sorrow think on him,
Together with remembrance of ourselves.
Therefore our sometime sister, now our queen,   8
Th' imperial jointress of this warlike state,
Have we, as 'twere with a defeated joy,
With an auspicious and a dropping eye,
With mirth in funeral and with dirge in marriage,   12
In equal scale weighing delight and dole,
Taken to wife. Nor have we herein barr'd
Your better wisdoms, which have freely gone
With this affair along. For all, our thanks.   16
Now follows that you know young Fortinbras,
Holding a weak supposal of our worth,

King tries to console Ham. 43 to marriage

I. ii. s.d. Flourish: *a trumpet call*   cum aliis; *cf. n.*
4 one brow of woe: *unanimity of sorrow*
9 jointress: *joint possessor*   10 defeated: *dispirited*
11 an auspicious: *one happy*   a dropping: *one tearful*
13 dole: *grief*   17 Now . . . know: *I must next inform you*
18 weak supposal: *low opinion*

Or thinking by our late dear brother's death
Our state to be disjoint and out of frame,   20
Colleagued with this dream of his advantage.
He hath not fail'd to pester us with message,
Importing the surrender of those lands
Lost by his father with all bands of law   24
To our most valiant brother. So much for him.
Now for ourself and for this time of meeting.
Thus much the business is: we have here writ
To Norway, uncle of young Fortinbras,   28
Who, impotent and bed-rid, scarcely hears
Of this his nephew's purpose, to suppress
His further gait herein in that the levies,
The lists and full proportions are all made   32
Out of his subject; and we here dispatch
You, good Cornelius, and you, Voltimand,
For bearers of this greeting to old Norway,
Giving to you no further personal power   36
To business with the king more than the scope
Of these delated articles allow.
Farewell and let your haste commend your duty.
    Cor. ⎱ In that and all things will we show our
    Vol. ⎰ duty.   40
    King. We doubt it nothing: heartily farewell.
                Exeunt Voltimand and Cornelius.

20 disjoint: *at loose ends*   frame: *order*
21 Colleagued . . . advantage: *conspired with himself to profit
    by this imaginary opportunity*
23 Importing: *bearing as its purport*   24 bands: *assurances*
31 gait: *proceeding*   in that: *because*
32 proportions: *supplies, forces*
33 his subject: *liegemen of Norway*
38 delated: *expressly stated*

And now, Laertes, what's the news with you?
You told us of some suit; what is't, Laertes?
You cannot speak of reason to the Dane,   44
And lose your voice. What wouldst thou beg, Laertes,
That shall not be my offer, not thy asking?
The head is not more native to the heart,
The hand more instrumental to the mouth,   48
Than is the throne of Denmark to thy father.
What wouldst thou have, Laertes?
    Laer.   Dread my lord,
Your leave and favor to return to France;
From whence though willingly I came to Denmark,   52
To show my duty in your coronation,
Yet now, I must confess, that duty done,
My thoughts and wishes bend again toward France
And bow them to your gracious leave and pardon.   56
    King. Have you your father's leave? What says Polo-
      nius?
    Pol. He hath, my lord, «wrung from me my slow leave
By laborsome petition, and at last
Upon his will I seal'd my hard consent».   60
I do beseech you, give him leave to go.
    King. Take thy fair hour, Laertes; time be thine,
And thy best graces spend it at thy will.
But now, my cousin Hamlet, and my son,—   64

45 lose your voice: *speak to no purpose*
47 native: *closely and congenitally connected*
48 instrumental: *serviceable*
50 Dread my lord: *my revered lord*
51 leave and favor: *kind permission*
56 leave and pardon: *indulgence* [*to depart*]
58–60 wrung, etc.; *not in Folio*
60 hard: *given with difficulty*
63 graces: *virtues*   64 cousin: *nephew*

Ham. [*Aside.*] A little more than kin, and less than
    kind.

King. How is it that the clouds still hang on you?

Ham. Not so, my lord; I am too much i' th' sun.

Queen. Good Hamlet, cast thy nighted color off,   68
And let thine eye look like a friend on Denmark.
Do not for ever with thy vailed lids
Seek for thy noble father in the dust.
Thou know'st 'tis common; all that lives must die,   72
Passing through nature to eternity.

Ham. Ay, madam, it is common.

Queen.   If it be,
Why seems it so particular with thee?

Ham. Seems, madam! Nay, it is; I know not 'seems.'   76
'Tis not alone my inky cloak, good mother,
Nor customary suits of solemn black,
Nor windy suspiration of forc'd breath,
No, nor the fruitful river in the eye,   80
Nor the dejected havior of the visage,
Together with all forms, moods, shapes of grief
That can denote me truly. These indeed seem,
For they are actions that a man might play: 84
But I have that within which passes show;
These but the trappings and the suits of woe.

King. 'Tis sweet and cómmendable in your nature,
    Hamlet,

65 kin . . . kind; *cf. n.*   67 i' th' sun; *cf. n.*
70 vailed: *down-cast*   72 common: *the common lot*
75 particular: *personal*
79 windy suspiration: *tempestuous sighing*   forc'd: *against*
    one's will
80 fruitful: *copious*
81 havior: *behavior*   83 denote: *portray*

To give these mourning duties to your father.   88
But, you must know, your father lost a father;
That father lost, lost his, and the survivor bound
In filial obligation for some term
To do obsequious sorrow; but to perséver   92
In obstinate condolement is a course
Of impious stubbornness; 'tis unmanly grief.
It shows a will most incorrect to heaven,
A heart unfortified, a mind impatient,   96
An understanding simple and unschool'd:
For what we know must be and is as common
As any the most vulgar thing to sense,
Why should we in our peevish opposition   100
Take it to heart? Fie! 'tis a fault to heaven,
A fault against the dead, a fault to nature,
To reason most absurd, whose common theme
Is death of fathers, and who still hath cried,   104
From the first corse till he that died to-day,
'This must be so.' We pray you, throw to earth
This unprevailing woe, and think of us
As of a father; for let the world take note,   108
You are the most immediate to our throne,
And with no less nobility of love
Than that which dearest father bears his son
Do I impórtune you. For your intent   112

90 bound: *was bound*   92 obsequious: *dutiful*
93 condolement: *sorrowing*
95 incorrect to: *unchastened toward*
99 vulgar . . . sense: *common experience*
105 corse: *corpse*
106 throw to earth: *drop (like a burden on one's back)*
107 unprevailing: *unavailing*
109 most immediate: *next in succession*
112 importune: *entreat; cf. n.*

In going back to school in Wittenberg,
It is most retrograde to our desire;
And we beseech you, bend you to remain
Here in the cheer and comfort of our eye,   116
Our chiefest courtier, cousin, and our son.
    Queen. Let not thy mother lose her prayers, Hamlet.
I pray thee, stay with us; go not to Wittenberg.
    Ham. I shall in all my best obey you, madam.   120
    King. Why, 'tis a loving and a fair reply!
Be as ourself in Denmark.—Madam, come.
This gentle and unforc'd accord of Hamlet
Sits smiling to my heart; in grace whereof,   124
No jocund health that Denmark drinks to-day,
But the great cannon to the clouds shall tell,
And the king's rouse the heavens shall bruit again,
Re-speaking earthly thunder. Come away.   128
           Flourish. Exeunt all but Hamlet.
    Ham. O that this too too solid flesh would melt,
Thaw and resolve itself into a dew!
Or that the Everlasting had not fix'd
His canon 'gainst self-slaughter! O God! God!   132
How weary, stale, flat, and unprofitable
Seem to me all the uses of this world.
Fie on 't! ah, fie! 'tis an unweeded garden,
That grows to seed; things rank and gross in nature   136
Possess it merely. That it should come to this!
But two months dead! nay, not so much, not two.
So excellent a king, that was to this

113 Wittenberg; *cf. n.*   114 retrograde: *contrary*
115 bend: *incline*
127 rouse: *revelry, 'carousing'*   bruit: *echo*
130 resolve: *dissolve*   132 canon: *divine law*
134 uses: *usages*   137 merely: *entirely*

Hyperion to a satyr; so loving to my mother   140
That he might not beteem the winds of heaven
Visit her face too roughly. Heaven and earth!
Must I remember? why, she would hang on him,
As if increase of appetite had grown   144
By what it fed on; and yet, within a month,—
Let me not think on 't! Frailty, thy name is woman.
A little month; or ere those shoes were old
With which she follow'd my poor father's body,
Like Niobe, all tears; why she,—   149
O God! a beast, that wants discourse of reason,
Would have mourn'd longer,—married with my uncle,
My father's brother, but no more like my father
Than I to Hercules. Within a month,   153
Ere yet the salt of most unrighteous tears
Had left the flushing in her galled eyes,
She married. O most wicked speed, to post
With such dexterity to incestuous sheets.   157
It is not, nor it cannot come to, good.—
But break, my heart, for I must hold my tongue.

Enter Horatio, Marcellus and Bernardo.

   Hor. Hail to your lordship!
   Ham.   I am glad to see you well.   160
Horatio! or I do forget myself.
   Hor. The same, my lord, and your poor servant ever.

140 Hyperion; *cf. n.*   141 beteem: *allow*
149 Niobe; *cf. n.*
150 discourse of reason: *reasoning power*
155 left the flushing: *ceased to produce redness*   galled: *sore
    with weeping*
156 post: *hasten*
157 dexterity: *facility*   161 forget myself; *cf. n.*

Ham. Sir, my good friend; I'll change that name with you.
And what make you from Wittenberg, Horatio?
Marcellus?   165
    Mar. My good lord,—
    Ham. I am very glad to see you. [*To Bernardo.*] Good even, sir.
But what, in faith, make you from Wittenberg?
    Hor. A truant disposition, good my lord.   169
    Ham. I would not hear your enemy say so,
Nor shall you do my ear that violence,
To make it truster of your own report   172
Against yourself; I know you are no truant.
But what is your affair in Elsinore?
We'll teach you to drink deep ere you depart.
    Hor. My lord, I came to see your father's funeral.   176
    Ham. I prithee, do not mock me, fellow-student.
I think it was to see my mother's wedding.
    Hor. Indeed, my lord, it follow'd hard upon.
    Ham. Thrift, thrift, Horatio! the funeral bak'd meats   180
Did coldly furnish forth the marriage tables.
Would I had met my dearest foe in heaven
Or ever I had seen that day, Horatio!
My father, methinks I see my father.   184
    Hor. Where, my lord?
    Ham.   In my mind's eye, Horatio.
    Hor. I saw him once; 'a was a goodly king.

163 change that name: *share the name of friend*
169 disposition: *temperament*
175 to drink deep; *cf. n.*
180 bak'd meats; *meat pies; cf. n.*   181 coldly: *when cold*
182 dearest: *direst*   183 Or: *before*

Horatio tells Hamlet has seen Hamlets father

Ham. 'A was a man! take him for all in all,
I shall not look upon his like again.   188
  Hor. My lord, I think I saw him yesternight.
  Ham. Saw? Who?
  Hor. My lord, the king your father.
  Ham.   The king, my father?
  Hor. Season your admiration for a while   192
With an attent ear, till I may deliver,
Upon the witness of these gentlemen,
This marvel to you.
  Ham.   For God's love, let me hear.
  Hor. Two nights together had these gentlemen,   196
Marcellus and Bernardo, on their watch,
In the dead waste and middle of the night,
Been thus encounter'd: a figure like your father,
Armed at point exactly, cap-a-pe,   200
Appears before them, and with solemn march
Goes slow and stately by them. Thrice he walk'd
By their oppress'd and fear-surprised eyes,
Within his truncheon's length; whilst they, distill'd 204
Almost to jelly with the act of fear,
Stand dumb and speak not to him. This to me
In dreadful secrecy impart they did,
And I with them the third night kept the watch;
Where, as they had deliver'd, both in time,   209
Form of the thing, each word made true and good,
The apparition comes. I knew your father;
These hands are not more like.

192 Season: *temper, qualify*   admiration: *wonder*
193 attent: *attentive*   198 waste; *cf. n.*
200 at point: *in full readiness*   cap-a-pe: *from head to foot*
204 truncheon: *officer's staff*   distill'd: *melted*
205 act: *operation*

Ham.   But where was this?

Mar. My lord, upon the platform where we
watch.   213

Ham. Did you not speak to it?

Hor.   My lord, I did;
But answer made it none; yet once methought
It lifted up it head and did address   216
Itself to motion, like as it would speak;
But even then the morning cock crew loud,
And at the sound it shrunk in haste away
And vanish'd from our sight.

Ham.   'Tis very strange.   220

Hor. As I do live, my honor'd lord, 'tis true;
And we did think it writ down in our duty
To let you know of it.

Ham. Indeed, indeed, sirs, but this troubles me.   224
Hold you the watch to-night?

All.   We do, my lord.

Ham. Arm'd, say you?

All.   Arm'd, my lord.

Ham.   From top to toe?

All. My lord, from head to foot.

Ham. Then saw you not his face.   228

Hor. O yes, my lord; he wore his beaver up.

Ham. What! look'd he frowningly?

Hor. A countenance more in sorrow than in anger.

Ham. Pale or red?   232

Hor. Nay, very pale.

Ham.   And fix'd his eyes upon you?

Hor. Most constantly.

Ham.   I would I had been there.

216 it: *its; cf. n.*   229 beaver: *face-guard of a helmet*

Hor. It would have much amaz'd you.

Ham.   Very like.   236
Stay'd it long?

Hor.   While one with moderate haste
Might tell a hundreth.

Both.   Longer, longer.

Hor. Not when I saw 't.

Ham.   His beard was grizzled, no?

Hor. It was, as I have seen it in his life,   240
A sable silver'd.

Ham.   I will watch to-night;
Perchance 'twill walk again.

Hor.   I warr'nt it will.

Ham. If it assume my noble father's person,
I'll speak to it, though hell itself should gape   244
And bid me hold my peace. I pray you all,
If you have hitherto conceal'd this sight,
Let it be tenable in your silence still;
And whatsomever else shall hap to-night,   248
Give it an understanding, but no tongue.
I will requite your loves. So, fare you well.
Upon the platform, 'twixt eleven and twelve,
I'll visit you.

All.   Our duty to your honor.   252

Ham. Your loves, as mine to you. Farewell.

                          Exeunt [all but Hamlet].
My father's spirit in arms! all is not well;
I doubt some foul play. Would the night were come!

238 tell: *count*   hundreth: *hundred (a Norse form)*
239 grizzled: *grey*
241 sable: *heraldic term for black*
247 Let . . . tenable: *see that you keep it*
248 whatsomever: *whatever*

Till then sit still, my soul: foul deeds will rise,   256
Though all the earth o'erwhelm them, to men's eyes.

Exit.

SCENE THIRD.

[*Polonius' Apartment in the Castle*]

Enter Laertes and Ophelia, his sister.

Laer. My necessaries are embark'd; farewell:
And, sister, as the winds give benefit
And convoy is assistant, do not sleep,
But let me hear from you.

Oph.   Do you doubt that?   4

Laer. For Hamlet, and the trifling of his favor,
Hold it a fashion and a toy in blood,
A violet in the youth of primy nature,
Forward, not permanent, sweet, not lasting,   8
The perfume and suppliance of a minute;
No more.

Oph.   No more but so?

Laer.   Think it no more:
For nature crescent does not grow alone
In thews and bulk, but as this temple waxes,   12
The inward service of the mind and soul
Grows wide withal. Perhaps he loves you now,

2 give benefit: *are favorable*   3 convoy: *means of conveyance*
6 fashion: *mere form*   toy in blood: *passing amorous fancy*
7 violet; *cf. n.*   primy: *spring-like*
8 Forward: *precocious*   9 suppliance: *diversion*
11 crescent: *growing*
12 thews: *bodily strength*   temple: *body*   14 withal: *also*

And now no soil nor cautel doth besmirch
The virtue of his will; but you must fear.   16
His greatness weigh'd, his will is not his own,
⟨For he himself is subject to his birth⟩.
He may not, as unvalu'd persons do,
Carve for himself, for on his choice depends   20
The safety and health of this whole state;
And therefore must his choice be circumscrib'd
Unto the voice and yielding of that body
Whereof he is the head. Then if he says he loves you,   24
It fits your wisdom so far to believe it
As he in his particular act and place
May give his saying deed; which is no further
Than the main voice of Denmark goes withal.   28
Then weigh what loss your honor may sustain,
If with too credent ear you list his songs,
Or lose your heart, or your chaste treasure open
To his unmaster'd importunity.   32
Fear it, Ophelia, fear it, my dear sister;
And keep you in the rear of your affection,
Out of the shot and danger of desire.
The chariest maid is prodigal enough   36
If she unmask her beauty to the moon;
Virtue itself 'scapes not calumnious strokes;
The canker galls the infants of the spring

15 soil: *blemish*   cautel: *trickery*
16 virtue of his will: *his virtuous intentions*
18 *not in Quarto*   19 unvalu'd: *untitled*
23 voice and yielding: *approval and compliance*
26 place: *position as a prince; cf. n.*   27 deed: *effect*
30 credent: *trustful*   list: *listen to*
32 unmaster'd: *unrestrained*   36 chariest: *most scrupulous*
39 canker: *caterpillar*   galls: *injures*   infants: *young plants*

Too oft before their buttons be disclos'd,   40
And in the morn and liquid dew of youth
Contagious blastments are most imminent.
Be wary then; best safety lies in fear:
Youth to itself rebels, though none else near.   44
    Oph. I shall the effect of this good lesson keep,
As watchman to my heart. But, good my brother,
Do not, as some ungracious pastors do,
Show me the steep and thorny way to heaven,
Whiles, like a puff'd and reckless libertine,   49
Himself the primrose path of dalliance treads,
And recks not his own rede.
    Laer.   O fear me not.

Enter Polonius.

I stay too long, but here my father comes.   52
A double blessing is a double grace;
Occasion smiles upon a second leave.
    Pol. Yet here, Laertes? aboard, aboard, for shame!
The wind sits in the shoulder of your sail,   56
And you are stay'd for. There, my blessing with thee!
And these few precepts in thy memory
Look thou charácter. Give thy thoughts no tongue,

40 buttons: *buds*   disclos'd: *opened*
41 liquid dew: *while the dew is still fresh*
42 blastments: *blights*   47 ungracious: *graceless*
49 puff'd: *bloated from excess*
50 primrose path: *path of pleasure*
51 recks: *heeds*   rede: *counsel*   fear me not: *don't worry
     about me*
53 double; cf. *n.*
54 Occasion: *opportunity*   smiles upon: *favors me with*
56 wind . . . of; cf. *n.*
58 precepts; cf. *n.*   59 character: *inscribe*

Nor any unproportion'd thought his act.   60
Be thou familiar, but by no means vulgar;
Those friends thou hast, and their adoption tried,
Grapple them unto thy soul with hoops of steel;
But do not dull thy palm with entertainment   64
Of each new-hatch'd, unfledg'd comráde. Beware
Of entrance to a quarrel, but, being in,
Bear 't that th' opposed may beware of thee.
Give every man thy ear, but few thy voice;   68
Take each man's censure, but reserve thy judgment.
Costly thy habit as thy purse can buy,
But not express'd in fancy; rich, not gaudy;
For the apparel oft proclaims the man,   72
And they in France of the best rank and station
Are of a most select and generous clef in that.
Neither a borrower, nor a lender be;
For loan oft loses both itself and friend,   76
And borrowing dulleth edge of husbandry.
This above all: to thine own self be true,
And it must follow, as the night the day,
Thou canst not then be false to any man.   80
Farewell; my blessing season this in thee!
    Laer. Most humbly do I take my leave, my lord.
    Pol. The time invites you; go, your servants tend.
    Laer. Farewell, Ophelia; and remember well
What I have said to you.

60 unproportion'd: *inordinate*   61 familiar: *friendly*
64 dull thy palm: *make yourself less sensitive to true friendship*
65 unfledg'd: *immature*   69 censure: *opinion*
71 express'd in fancy: *singular in design*
74 generous: *aristocratic*   clef: *musical key, tone; cf. n.*
77 husbandry: *thrift*
81 season this: *make my admonition palatable*
83 tend: *are in waiting*

Oph.   'Tis in my memory lock'd,
And you yourself shall keep the key of it.   86
    Laer. Farewell.   *Exit Laertes.*
    Pol. What is 't, Ophelia, he hath said to you?
    Oph. So please you, something touching the Lord
    Hamlet.
    Pol. Marry, well bethought:
'Tis told me, he hath very oft of late
Given private time to you; and you yourself   92
Have of your audience been most free and bounteous.
If it be so,—as so 'tis put on me,
And that in way of caution,—I must tell you,
You do not understand yourself so clearly   96
As it behoves my daughter and your honor.
What is between you? give me up the truth.
    Oph. He hath, my lord, of late made many tenders
Of his affection to me.   100
    Pol. Affection! pooh! you speak like a green girl,
Unsifted in such perilous circumstance.
Do you believe his tenders, as you call them?
    Oph. I do not know, my lord, what I should
    think.   104
    Pol. Marry, I'll teach you: think yourself a baby,
That you have ta'en these tenders for true pay,
Which are not sterling. Tender yourself more dearly;
Or (not to crack the wind of the poor phrase,
Running it thus) you'll tender me a fool.   109

92 private time: *time in private visits*
94 put on: *impressed on*
99 tenders: *offers; cf. n.*
101 green: *inexperienced*
102 Unsifted: *untried*   circumstance: *state of affairs*
107 sterling: *legal currency*   109 Running; *cf. n.*

Oph. My lord, he hath impórtun'd me with love
In honorable fashion.

Pol. Ay, fashion you may call it. Go to, go to.   112

Oph. And hath given countenance to his speech, my
lord,
With almost all the holy vows of heaven.

Pol. Ay, springes to catch woodcocks. I do know,
When the blood burns, how prodigal the soul   116
Lends the tongue vows: these blazes, daughter,
Giving more light than heat, extinct in both,
Even in their promise, as it is a-making,
You must not take for fire. From this time   120
Be somewhat scanter of your maiden presence;
Set your entreatments at a higher rate
Than a command to parley. For Lord Hamlet,
Believe so much in him: that he is young,   124
And with a larger tether may he walk
Than may be given you. In few, Ophelia,
Do not believe his vows, for they are brokers,
Not of that dye which their investments show,
But mere implorators of unholy suits,   129
Breathing like sanctified and pious bawds,
The better to beguile. This is for all:
I would not, in plain terms, from this time forth,
Have you so slander any moment leisure,   133
As to give words or talk with the Lord Hamlet.
Look to 't, I charge you; come your ways.

Oph. I shall obey, my lord.   *Exeunt.*

115 springes: *snares*   woodcocks; *cf. n.*
122 entreatments: *interviews*   126 In few: *briefly*
127 brokers: *go-betweens, procurers*
128 investments: *vestments, clothes*   129 implorators: *solicitors*
130 bawds; *cf. n.*   133 slander: *bring reproach upon*

[SCENE FOURTH.

The Platform of the Castle]

Enter Hamlet, Horatio, and Marcellus.

Ham. The air bites shrewdly; it is very cold.
Hor. It is a nipping and an eager air.
Ham. What hour now?
Hor.   I think it lacks of twelve.
Mar. No, it is struck.   4
Hor. Indeed? I heard it not: it then draws near the
   season
Wherein the spirit held his wont to walk.
      A flourish of trumpets, and two pieces [*of*
               ordnance] *go off.*
What does this mean, my lord?
   Ham. The king doth wake to-night and takes his
      rouse,   8
Keeps wassail, and the swaggering up-spring reels;
And, as he drains his draughts of Rhenish down,
The kettle-drum and trumpet thus bray out
The triumph of his pledge.
   Hor.   Is it a custom?   12
   Ham. Ay, marry, is 't:
But to my mind, though I am native here
And to the manner born, it is a custom
More honor'd in the breach than the observance.   16

---

2 eager: *sharp*   8 wake: *hold a revel by night*
9 Keeps wassail: *holds a drinking-bout*   up-spring: *wild dance*
   of German origin
10 Rhenish: *Rhine wine*   12 pledge: *toast*

«This heavy-headed revel east and west
Makes us traduc'd and tax'd of other nations;
They clepe us drunkards, and with swinish phrase
Soil our addition; and indeed it takes   20
From our achievements, though perform'd at height,
The pith and marrow of our attribute.
So, oft it chances in particular men,
That for some vicious mole of nature in them,   24
As, in their birth, (wherein they are not guilty,
Since nature cannot choose his origin),
By the o'ergrowth of some complexion,
Oft breaking down the pales and forts of reason,   28
Or by some habit that too much o'er-leavens
The form of plausive manners; that these men,
Carrying, I say, the stamp of one defect,
Being nature's livery, or fortune's star,—   32
His virtues else, be they as pure as grace,
As infinite as man may undergo,
Shall in the general censure take corruption
From that particular fault. The dram of eale   36
Doth all the noble substance oft adulter
To his own scandal.»

17-38 *Not in Folio*
18 traduc'd and tax'd: *defamed and censured*
19 clepe: *call*   swinish phrase: *name of 'pigs'*
20 Soil our addition: *blemish our good name*
21 at height: *to the maximum*   22 attribute: *reputation*
24 mole: *blemish*   27 complexion: *natural tendency, 'humor'*
28 pales: *defensive enclosures*
29 o'er-leavens: *makes too light*   30 plausive: *pleasing*
32 nature's livery: *a natural attribute*   fortune's star: *the position in which one is placed by fortune*
33 His; *cf. n.*   34 undergo: *bear the weight of*
36 dram: *minute quantity*   eale: *e'il, evil*
37 oft adulter; *cf. n.*   38 scandal: *shame*

Ghost entreats Hamlet to private conference

Enter Ghost.

Hor.   Look, my lord, it comes!

Ham. Angels and ministers of grace defend us!
Be thou a spirit of health or goblin damn'd,   40
Bring with thee airs from heaven or blasts from hell,
Be thy intents wicked or charitable,
Thou com'st in such a questionable shape
That I will speak to thee. I'll call thee Hamlet,   44
King, father, royal Dane! O answer me:
Let me not burst in ignorance, but tell
Why thy canóniz'd bones, hearsed in death,
Have burst their cerements; why the sepulchre,   48
Wherein we saw thee quietly inurn'd,
Hath op'd his ponderous and marble jaws,
To cast thee up again? What may this mean,
That thou, dead corse, again in cómplete steel   52
Revisits thus the glimpses of the moon,
Making night hideous; and we fools of nature
So horridly to-shake our disposition
With thoughts beyond the reaches of our souls?   56
Say, why is this? wherefore? what should we do?

                              Ghost beckons Hamlet.

39 ministers of grace: *messengers of God*
40 spirit of health: *good spirit*   goblin: *evil spirit*
43 questionable: *inviting question*
47 canoniz'd: *buried according to the Church's rule*   hearsed:
    coffined
48 cerements: *waxen grave-clothes*
49 inurn'd: *interred; cf. n.*
53 glimpses of the moon: *the earth by night*
54 fools of nature: *stupid in nature's presence*
55 to-shake our disposition: *shatter our composure*
56 reaches: *capacities*

Hor. It beckons you to go away with it,
As if it some impartment did desire
To you alone.
Mar.   Look, with what courteous action   60
It waves you to a more removed ground:
But do not go with it.
Hor.   No, by no means.
Ham. It will not speak. Then, I will follow it.
Hor. Do not, my lord.
Ham.   Why, what should be the fear?   64
I do not set my life at a pin's fee;
And for my soul, what can it do to that,
Being a thing immortal as itself?
It waves me forth again; I'll follow it.   68
Hor. What if it tempt you toward the flood, my lord,
Or to the dreadful summit of the cliff
That beetles o'er his base into the sea,
And there assume some other horrible form,   72
Which might deprive your sovereignty of reason
And draw you into madness? think of it;
«The very place puts toys of desperation,
Without more motive, into every brain   76
That looks so many fadoms to the sea
And hears it roar beneath.»

59 impartment: *communication*
65 at . . . fee: *at even a trifling value*
69 flood: *sea*   71 beetles: *overhangs threateningly*
73 deprive . . . reason: *dethrone reason from its sovereignty*
75–78 The . . . beneath; *not in Folio*
75 toys of desperation: *whims involving thoughts of self-destruction*
77 fadoms: *fathoms*

Ham. It waves me still. Go on! I'll follow thee.
Mar. You shall not go, my lord.
Ham.   Hold off your hands!   80
Hor. Be rul'd; you shall not go.
Ham.   My fate cries out,
And makes each petty arture in this body
As hardy as the Némean lion's nerve.
Still am I call'd. Unhand me, gentlemen!   84
By heaven, I'll make a ghost of him that lets me.
I say, away!—Go on! I'll follow thee.

                              Exeunt Ghost and Hamlet.

Hor. He waxes desperate with imagination.
Mar. Let's follow; 'tis not fit thus to obey him.   88
Hor. Have after. To what issue will this come?
Mar. Something is rotten in the state of Denmark.
Hor. Heaven will direct it.
Mar.   Nay, let's follow him.

                              Exeunt.

[SCENE FIFTH.

A more remote Part of the Platform]

Enter Ghost and Hamlet.

Ham. Whither wilt thou lead me? speak; I'll go no
   further.
Ghost. Mark me.
Ham.   I will.

82 arture: *artery*
83 Nemean lion's; *cf. n.*   nerve: *sinew, tendon*
85 lets: *hinders*   89 issue: *outcome*

Ghost. My hour is almost come,
When I to sulphurous and tormenting flames
Must render up myself.

Ham. Alas, poor ghost. 4

Ghost. Pity me not, but lend thy serious hearing
To what I shall unfold.

Ham. Speak; I am bound to hear.

Ghost. So art thou to revenge, when thou shalt hear.

Ham. What? 8

Ghost. I am thy father's spirit,
Doom'd for a certain term to walk the night,
And for the day confin'd to fast in fires,
Till the foul crimes done in my days of nature 12
Are burnt and purg'd away. But that I am forbid
To tell the secrets of my prison-house,
I could a tale unfold whose lightest word
Would harrow up thy soul, freeze thy young blood, 16
Make thy two eyes, like stars, start from their spheres,
Thy knotted and combined locks to part,
And each particular hair to stand an end,
Like quills upon the fretful porpentine. 20
But this eternal blazon must not be
To ears of flesh and blood. List, list, oh list!
If thou didst ever thy dear father love—

Ham. O God! 24

Ghost. Revenge his foul and most unnatural murther.

Ham. Murther!

17 spheres: *orbits*
18 knotted: *neatly arranged*   combined: *smoothly combed*
19 an: *on*
20 porpentine: *porcupine*
21 eternal blazon: *revelation of eternity; cf. n.*
25 unnatural: i.e., *for one brother to kill another*

Ghost. Murther most foul, as in the best it is;
But this most foul, strange, and unnatural.   28

Ham. Haste me to know 't, that I, with wings as swift
As meditation or the thoughts of love,
May sweep to my revenge.

Ghost.   I find thee apt;
And duller shouldst thou be than the fat weed   32
That roots itself in ease on Lethe wharf,
Wouldst thou not stir in this. Now, Hamlet, hear:
'Tis given out that, sleeping in my orchard,
A serpent stung me. So the whole ear of Denmark   36
Is by a forged process of my death
Rankly abus'd; but know, thou noble youth,
The serpent that did sting thy father's life
Now wears his crown.

Ham.   O my prophetic soul!   40
My uncle?

Ghost. Ay, that incestuous, that adulterate beast,
With witchcraft of his wit, with traitorous gifts,—
O wicked wit and gifts, that have the power   44
So to seduce!—won to his shameful lust
The will of my most seeming-virtuous queen.
O Hamlet, what a falling-off was there!
From me, whose love was of that dignity   48
That it went hand in hand even with the vow
I made to her in marriage; and to decline
Upon a wretch whose natural gifts were poor

31 apt: *ready to learn*   32 fat weed; *cf. n.*
33 Lethe; *cf. n.*   wharf: *bank*
35 orchard: *garden*   37 process: *narrative*
38 abus'd: *deceived*   42 adulterate: *adulterous*

To those of mine! 52
But virtue, as it never will be mov'd,
Though lewdness court it in a shape of heaven,
So lust, though to a radiant angel link'd,
Will sate itself in a celestial bed, 56
And prey on garbage.
But, soft! methinks I scent the morning air;
Brief let me be. Sleeping within my orchard,
My custom always of the afternoon, 60
Upon my secure hour thy uncle stole,
With juice of cursed hebona in a vial,
And in the porches of my ears did pour
The leperous distilment; whose effect 64
Holds such an enmity with blood of man
That swift as quicksilver it courses through
The natural gates and alleys of the body,
And with a sudden vigor it doth posset 68
And curd, like eager droppings into milk,
The thin and wholesome blood. So did it mine;
And a most instant tetter bark'd about,
Most lazar-like, with vile and loathsome crust,
All my smooth body. 73
Thus was I, sleeping, by a brother's hand,
Of life, of crown, of queen, at once dispatch'd;
Cut off even in the blossoms of my sin, 76

62 hebona: *yew, notorious for its poisonous properties, but hen-
bane and ebony are also involved*
64 leperous: *causing leprosy* 67 gates and alleys: *streets and
lanes; cf. n.* 68 posset: *curdle* 69 eager: *sour*
71 instant: *instantaneous* tetter: *skin eruption* bark'd
about: *covered (as with bark)*
72 lazar-like: *leprous-like* 75 dispatch'd: *bereft*

Unhousel'd, disappointed, unanel'd,
No reckoning made, but sent to my account
With all my imperfections on my head.
[*Ham.*] O horrible! O horrible! most horrible!   80
[*Ghost.*] If thou hast nature in thee, bear it not;
Let not the royal bed of Denmark be
A couch for luxury and damned incest.
But, howsomever thou pursu'st this act,   84
Taint not thy mind, nor let thy soul contrive
Against thy mother aught. Leave her to heaven,
And to those thorns that in her bosom lodge,
To prick and sting her. Fare thee well at once!   88
The glow-worm shows the matin to be near,
And 'gins to pale his uneffectual fire;
Adieu, adieu, adieu! Remember me.   *Exit.*
    Ham. O all you host of heaven! O earth! What else?   92
And shall I couple hell? O fie! Hold, hold, my heart!
And you, my sinews, grow not instant old,
But bear me stiffly up. Remember thee?
Ay, thou poor ghost, while memory holds a seat   96
In this distracted globe. Remember thee?
Yea, from the table of my memory
I'll wipe away all trivial fond records,
All saws of books, all forms, all pressures past,   100
That youth and observation copied there;

77 Unhousel'd: *without having received the Holy Communion*
    disappointed: *unprepared*   unanel'd: *without having re-
    ceived extreme unction*
78 reckoning: *confession and absolution*   80 O horrible; *cf. n.*
83 luxury: *lasciviousness*   89 matin: *morning*
90 uneffectual: *heatless*   97 distracted globe: *confused head*
98 table: *writing-tablet*   99 fond: *foolish*
100 saws: *maxims*   pressures: *impressions—as of a seal*

And thy commandment all alone shall live
Within the book and volume of my brain,
Unmix'd with baser matter: yes, by heaven!   104
O most pernicious woman!
O villain, villain, smiling, damned villain!
My tables! Meet it is I set it down,
That one may smile, and smile, and be a villain;   108
At least I'm sure it may be so in Denmark.

                             [Writing.]

So, uncle, there you are. Now to my word.
It is, 'Adieu, adieu! remember me.'
I have sworn 't.   112
    Hor. and Mar. within. My lord! my lord!

        Enter Horatio and Marcellus.

Mar.   Lord Hamlet!
Hor. Heaven secure him!
Ham.   So be it!
Hor. Illo, ho, ho, my lord!
Ham. Hillo, ho, ho, boy! come, bird, come.
Mar. How is 't, my noble lord?
Hor.   What news, my lord?   117
Ham. O wonderful!
Hor.   Good my lord, tell it.
Ham. No; you will reveal it.
Hor. Not I, my lord, by heaven!
Mar.   Nor I, my lord.   120
Ham. How say you, then? would heart of man once
    think it?

110 word: *watch-word*
115 Illo, ho, ho: *falconer's hunting call*
116 come, bird, come: *call which falconers use to their hawk in the air*

But you'll be secret?

Both.   Ay, by heaven, my lord.

Ham. <u>There's ne'er a villain dwelling in all Denmark,</u>
But he 's an arrant knave.   124

Hor. There needs no ghost, my lord, come from the
    grave,
To tell us this.

Ham.   Why, right; you are in the right;
And so, without more circumstance at all,
I hold it fit that we shake hands and part;   128
You, as your business and desire shall point you,—
For every man hath business and desire,
Such as it is,—and, for my own poor part,
I will go pray.   132

Hor. <u>These are but wild and whirling words, my lord.</u>

Ham. I am sorry they offend you, heartily;
Yes, faith, heartily.

Hor.   There's no offence, my lord.

Ham. Yes, by Saint Patrick, but there is, Horatio,   136
And much offence, too. Touching this vision here,
It is an honest ghost, that let me tell you.
For your desire to know what is between us,
O'ermaster 't as you may. And now, good friends,   140
As you are friends, scholars, and soldiers,
Give me one poor request.

Hor. What is 't, my lord? we will.

Ham. <u>Never make known what you have seen to-
    night.</u>   144

Both. My lord, we will not.

---

124 arrant: *thoroughgoing*	127 circumstance: *formality*
133 whirling: *eddying, incoherent*	136 Saint Patrick; *cf. n.*
138 honest ghost; *cf. n.*	140 O'ermaster 't: *conquer it*

Ham.   Nay, but swear 't.

Hor.   In faith,
My lord, not I.

     Mar.   Nor I, my lord, in faith.

     Ham. Upon my sword.

     Mar.   We have sworn, my lord, already.

     Ham. Indeed, upon my sword, indeed.   148

     Ghost. Swear.   *Ghost cries under the stage.*

     Ham. Ha, ha, boy! sayst thou so? art thou there, true-
penny?
Come on,—you hear this fellow in the cellarage,—
Consent to swear.

     Hor.   Propose the oath, my lord.   152

     Ham. Never to speak of this that you have seen.
Swear by my sword.

     Ghost. Swear.

     Ham. Hic et ubique? then we'll shift our ground.   156
Come hither, gentlemen, and lay your hands
Again upon my sword. Swear by my sword
Never to speak of this that you have heard.

     Ghost. Swear by his sword.   160

     Ham. Well said, old mole! canst work i' th' earth so fast?
A worthy pioner! once more remove, good friends.

     Hor. O day and night, but this is wondrous strange!

     Ham. And therefore as a stranger give it welcome.   164
There are more things in heaven and earth, Horatio,
Than are dreamt of in your philosophy.
But come;
Here, as before, never, so help you mercy,   168

---

150 true-penny: *honest fellow*   154 sword; *cf. n.*
156 *Hic et ubique:* here and everywhere
162 pioner: *digger, miner*   166 your; *cf. n.*

How strange or odd soe'er I bear myself,—
As I perchance hereafter shall think meet
To put an antic disposition on,—
That you, at such times seeing me, never shall,   172
With arms encumber'd thus, or this head-shake,
Or by pronouncing of some doubtful phrase,
As, 'Well, well, we know,' or, 'We could, an if we would;'
Or, 'If we list to speak,' or, 'There be, an if they
    might;'   176
Or such ambiguous giving out, to note
That you know aught of me. This do swear,
So grace and mercy at your most need help you.
    Ghost. Swear.   [*They swear.*]
    Ham. Rest, rest, perturbed spirit! So, gentlemen, 181
With all my love I do commend me to you:
And what so poor a man as Hamlet is
May do t' express his love and friending to you,   184
God willing, shall not lack. Let us go in together;
And still your fingers on your lips, I pray.
The time is out of joint. O cursed spite,
That ever I was born to set it right!   188
Nay, come, let's go together.   *Exeunt.*

170 meet: *proper*   171 antic: *fantastic*
173 encumber'd: *folded; cf. n.*   174 doubtful: *ambiguous*
176 an if: *an intensive form of if*
177 to note: *to give a sign*   187 spite: *vexatious circumstance*

If Hamlet acts mad he tells his
friends never to laugh or
scorn him.

ACT SECOND

[SCENE FIRST.

Polonius' Apartment in the Castle]

Enter old Polonius with his man [Reynaldo].

Pol. Give him this money and these notes, Reynaldo.
Rey. I will, my lord.
Pol. You shall do marvel's wisely, good Reynaldo,
Before you visit him, to make inquire   4
Of his behavior.
Rey.   My lord, I did intend it.
Pol. Marry, well said, very well said. Look you, sir,
Inquire me first what Danskers are in Paris;
And how, and who, what means, and where they
     keep,   8
What company, at what expense; and finding
By this encompassment and drift of question
That they do know my son, come you more nearer
Than your particular demands will touch it.   12
Take you, as 'twere, some distant knowledge of him;
As thus, 'I know his father, and his friends,
And in part him.' Do you mark this, Reynaldo?

1 notes: *instructions*
3 marvel's: *marvelously*   4 inquire: *investigation*
7 Danskers: *Danes*   8 keep: *live*
10 encompassment: *'talking round' a subject*   question: *conversation*
12 particular demands: *concrete questions*   13 Take: *assume*

Rey. Ay, very well, my lord.   16

Pol. 'And in part him; but,' you may say, 'not well:
But if 't be he I mean, he's very wild,
Addicted so and so'; and there put on him
What forgeries you please: marry, none so rank
As may dishonor him; take heed of that;   21
But, sir, such wanton, wild, and usual slips
As are companions noted and most known
To youth and liberty.

Rey.   As gaming, my lord?   24

Pol. Ay, or drinking, fencing, swearing,
Quarrelling, drabbing,—you may go so far.

Rey. My lord, that would dishonor him.

Pol. Faith, no, as you may season it in the charge.   28
You must not put another scandal on him,
That he is open to incontinency.
That's not my meaning; but breathe his faults so quaintly
That they may seem the taints of liberty,   32
The flash and outbreak of a fiery mind,
A savageness in unreclaimed blood,
Of general assault.

Rey.   But, my good lord,—

Pol. Wherefore should you do this?

Rey.   Ay, my lord,   36
I would know that.

19 put on: *impute to*
20 forgeries: *invented tales*   rank: *excessive*
22 wanton: *unrestrained*   26 drabbing: *wenching*
28 season: *flavor*   charge: *accusation*
30 incontinency: *habitual loose behavior*
31 breathe . . . quaintly: *hint . . . cleverly*
32 taints of liberty: *blemishes due to high spirits*
34 savageness: *wildness*   unreclaimed: *untamed*
35 Of general assault: *to which all are liable*

Pol.   Marry, sir, here's my drift;
And I believe it is a fetch of warrant.
You laying these slight sullies on my son,
As 'twere a thing a little soil'd i' th' working,   40
Mark you,
Your party in converse, him you would sound,
Having ever seen in the prenominate crimes
The youth you breathe of guilty, be assur'd,   44
He closes with you in this consequence:
'Good sir,' or so, or 'friend,' or 'gentleman,'
According to the phrase or the addition
Of man and country—
Rey.   Very good, my lord.   48
     Pol. And then, sir, does 'a this,—'a does,—what was
I about to say? By the mass I was about to say some-
thing. Where did I leave?
     Rey. At 'closes in the consequence,'   52
At 'friend or so,' and 'gentleman.'
     Pol. At 'closes in the consequence'? Ay, marry;
He closes thus: 'I know the gentleman;
I saw him yesterday, or th' other day,   56
Or then, or then, with such or such; and, as you say,
There was 'a gaming, there o'ertook in 's rouse,
There falling out at tennis'; or perchance,
'I saw him enter such a house of sale,'   60
Videlicet, a brothel, or so forth.
See you now;

38 fetch of warrant: *justifiable trick*   39 sullies: *blemishes*
40 *Cf. n.*   43 prenominate: *aforesaid*
45 closes . . . consequence: *confides in you as follows*
51 leave: *leave off*
58 o'ertook in 's rouse: *unable to hold his liquor*
61 *Videlicet:* namely

Your bait of falsehood takes this carp of truth;
And thus do we of wisdom and of reach, 64
With windlasses and with assays of bias,
By indirections find directions out.
So by my former lecture and advice
Shall you my son. You have me, have you not? 68
   Rey. My lord, I have.
   Pol.   God be wi' ye; fare ye well.
   Rey. Good my lord!
   Pol. Observe his inclination in yourself.
   Rey. I shall, my lord. 72
   Pol. And let him ply his music.
   Rey.   Well, my lord.
   Pol. Farewell!   *Exit Reynaldo.*

Enter Ophelia.

           How now, Ophelia! what's the matter?
   Oph. O my lord, my lord! I have been so affrighted.
   Pol. With what, i' th' name of God? 76
   Oph. My lord, as I was sewing in my closet,
Lord Hamlet, with his doublet all unbrac'd,
No hat upon his head; his stockings foul'd,
Ungarter'd, and down-gyved to his ankle;— 80
Pale as his shirt, his knees knocking each other,

64 reach: *resourcefulness*
65 windlasses: *roundabout ways*   assays of bias: *indirect approaches*
66 indirections: *devious courses*   directions: *the straight facts*
67 lecture: *instruction*   71 in yourself: *for yourself*
73 ply: *keep up*   77 closet: *sitting room*
78 doublet: *close-fitting coat*   unbrac'd: *unfastened*
80 down-gyved: *hanging down like gyves or fetters*

And with a look so piteous in purport
As if he had been loosed out of hell
To speak of horrors, he comes before me.   84
  Pol. Mad for thy love?
  Oph.   My lord, I do not know;
But truly I do fear it.
  Pol.   What said he?
  Oph. He took me by the wrist and held me hard,
Then goes he to the length of all his arm,   88
And, with his other hand thus o'er his brow,
He falls to such perusal of my face
As 'a would draw it. Long stay'd he so.
At last, a little shaking of mine arm,   92
And thrice his head thus waving up and down,
He rais'd a sigh so piteous and profound
As it did seem to shatter all his bulk
And end his being. That done, he lets me go,   96
And with his head over his shoulder turn'd,
He seem'd to find his way without his eyes,
For out o' doors he went without their help,
And to the last bended their light on me.   100
  Pol. Come, go with me. I will go seek the king.
This is the very ecstasy of love,
Whose violent property fordoes itself
And leads the will to desperate undertakings   104
As oft as any passion under heaven
That does afflict our natures. I am sorry.
What! have you given him any hard words of late?

90 perusal: *scrutiny*
95 bulk: *frame*   102 ecstasy: *madness*
103 property: *nature*   fordoes: *destroys*

Oph. No, my good lord; but, as you did command,   108
I did repel his letters and denied
His access to me.
    Pol.   That hath made him mad.
I am sorry that with better heed and judgment
I had not coted him. I fear'd he did but trifle,   112
And meant to wrack thee, but beshrew my jealousy!
By heaven, it is as proper to our age
To cast beyond ourselves in our opinions
As it is common for the younger sort   116
To lack discretion. Come, go we to the king.
This must be known, which, being kept close, might move
More grief to hide than hate to utter love.
Come.   *Exeunt.*

SCENE SECOND.

[*The Lobby in the Castle*]

*Flourish. Enter King and Queen, Rosencrantz and
Guildenstern, cum aliis.*

King. Welcome, dear Rosencrantz and Guildenstern.
Moreover that we much did long to see you,
The need we have to use you did provoke
Our hasty sending. Something have you heard   4

112 coted: *observed (obsolete form of 'quote')*
113 wrack: *ruin*   beshrew: *curse*   jealousy: *suspicion, mis-
    trust*
114 our age: *us old folk*
115 cast . . . ourselves: *be over subtle*
119 More . . . love; *cf. n.*

[handwritten marginalia, left side:] Polonius goes to king with solution for Hamlet's madness.

[handwritten marginalia, lower left:] King welcomes Ros + Guilde to spy on him. Gives excuse for Hamlet's own benefit

Of Hamlet's transformation. So I call it,
Sith nor th' exterior nor the inward man
Resembles that it was. What it should be,
More than his father's death, that thus hath put him   8
So much from th' understanding of himself,
I cannot dream of. I entreat you both,
That being of so young days brought up with him,
And since so neighbor'd to his youth and havior,   12
That you vouchsafe your rest here in our court
Some little time; so by your companies
To draw him on to pleasures and to gather,
So much as from occasion you may glean,   16
«Whether aught to us unknown afflicts him thus,»
That, open'd, lies within our remedy.

   Queen. Good gentlemen, he hath much talk'd of you;
And sure I am two men there are not living   20
To whom he more adheres. If it will please you
To show us so much gentry and good will
As to expend your time with us awhile,
For the supply and profit of our hope,   24
Your visitation shall receive such thanks
As fits a king's remembrance.

   Ros.   Both your majesties
Might, by the sovereign power you have of us,
Put your dread pleasures more into command
Than to entreaty.

   Guil.   But we both obey,   29

11 of so young days: *from such early youth; cf. n.*
12 neighbor'd . . . havior: *near in age and occupation*
13 vouchsafe your rest: *please to reside*   17 *not in Folio*
18 open'd: *revealed*   22 gentry: *courtesy*
24 supply and profit: *aid and successful outcome*
26 as . . . remembrance: *as is suitable to a king's gratitude*

And here give up ourselves in the full bent,
To lay our service freely at your feet
To be commanded.   32
   King. Thanks, Rosencrantz and gentle Guildenstern.
   Queen. Thanks, Guildenstern and gentle Rosencrantz;
And I beseech you instantly to visit
My too much changed son. Go, some of you,   36
And bring these gentlemen where Hamlet is.
   Guil. Heavens make our presence and our practices
Pleasant and helpful to him!
   Queen.   Ay, amen!
          Exeunt Rosencrantz and Guildenstern [attended].

Enter Polonius.

   Pol. Th' ambassadors from Norway, my good lord,   40
Are joyfully return'd.
   King. Thou still hast been the father of good news.
   Pol. Have I, my lord? Assure you, my good liege,
I hold my duty as I hold my soul,   44
Both to my God and to my gracious king;
And I do think—or else this brain of mine
Hunts not the trail of policy so sure
As it hath us'd to do—that I have found   48
The very cause of Hamlet's lunacy.
   King. O speak of that! that do I long to hear.
   Pol. Give first admittance to th' ambassadors;
My news shall be the fruit to that great feast.   52
   King. Thyself do grace to them, and bring them in.
                 [Exit Polonius.]

30 in the full bent: *to the utmost degree (an archery term)*
44, 45 *Cf. n.*
47 policy: *conduct of public affairs*   52 fruit: *dessert*

He tells me, my dear Gertrude, he hath found
The head and source of all your son's distemper.
    Queen. I doubt it is no other but the main: 56
His father's death and our o'erhasty marriage.
    King. Well, we shall sift him.

Enter Polonius, Voltimand, and Cornelius.

                  Welcome, my good friends!
Say, Voltimand, what from our brother Norway?
    Volt. Most fair return of greetings and desires.   60
Upon our first, he sent out to suppress
His nephew's levies, which to him appear'd
To be a preparation 'gainst the Polack;
But, better look'd into, he truly found   64
It was against your highness: whereat griev'd
That so his sickness, age, and impotence
Was falsely borne in hand, sends out arrests
On Fortinbras; which he in brief obeys,   68
Receives rebuke from Norway, and, in fine,
Makes vow before his uncle never more
To give th' assay of arms against your majesty.
Whereon old Norway, overcome with joy,   72
Gives him three thousand crowns in annual fee,
And his commission to employ those soldiers,
So levied as before, against the Polack;
With an entreaty, herein further shown,   76
                [*Giving a paper.*]
That it might please you to give quiet pass

56 main: *chief point*   60 desires: *good wishes*
61 Upon our first; *cf. n.*   67 borne in hand: *deluded*
69 in fine: *in conclusion*   71 assay: *trial*
73 *Cf. n.*   74 his commission; *cf. n.*

Through your dominions for this enterprise,
On such regards of safety and allowance
As therein are set down.

    King.   It likes us well;   80
And at our more consider'd time we'll read,
Answer, and think upon this business.
Meantime we thank you for your well-took labor.
Go to your rest; at night we'll feast together.
Most welcome home.

                          Exeunt Ambassadors.

    Pol.   This business is well ended.   85
My liege, and madam, to expostulate
What majesty should be, what duty is,
Why day is day, night night, and time is time,
Were nothing but to waste night, day, and time.
Therefore, since brevity is the soul of wit,
And tediousness the limbs and outward flourishes,
I will be brief. Your noble son is mad.   92
Mad call I it; for to define true madness,
What is 't but to be nothing else but mad?
But let that go.

    Queen.   More matter, with less art.
    Pol. Madam, I swear I use no art at all.   96
That he is mad, 'tis true; 'tis true 'tis pity;
And pity 'tis 'tis true: a foolish figure,
But farewell it, for I will use no art.
Mad let us grant him, then; and now remains
That we find out the cause of this effect,   101

79 regards . . . allowance; *cf. n.*   80 likes: *pleases*
81 consider'd: *fit for considering*
86 expostulate: *set forth one's views*
90 wit: *judgment, understanding*
91 flourishes: *embellishments*   98 figure: *figure of rhetoric*

[handwritten marginal note: This is Polonius' brevity! We have lost all the original respect for him]

*Polonius reads Hamlet's love letters
to Ophelia + King + Queen to prove this
is reason for his madness*

II:2   Prince of Denmark   57

Or rather say, the cause of this defect,
For this effect defective comes by cause.
Thus it remains, and the remainder thus.
Perpend.   105
I have a daughter (have while she is mine)
Who, in her duty and obedience, mark,
Hath given me this. Now, gather and surmise.

                    [*Reads*] *The Letter.*

To the celestial, and my soul's idol, the most beautified Ophe-
    lia.—   109

    That's an ill phrase, a vile phrase; 'beautified' is a
    vile phrase; but you shall hear. Thus:

In her excellent white bosom, these, &c.—   112

    Queen. Came this from Hamlet to her?
    Pol. Good madam, stay awhile; I will be faithful.

            Doubt thou the stars are fire;
                Doubt that the sun doth move;   116
            Doubt truth to be a liar;
                But never doubt I love.
        O dear Ophelia! I am ill at these numbers: I have
    not art to reckon my groans; but that I love thee best,
    O most best, believe it. Adieu.
                Thine evermore, most dear lady, whilst this
                    machine is to him,

                            Hamlet.

This in obedience hath my daughter shown me,   125
And more above,—hath his solicitings,

105 Perpend: *consider*
109 beautified: *beautiful, or, accomplished*   112 these; *cf. n.*
119 ill at: *unskilled at making*   numbers: *verses*
120 reckon: *number metrically, scan*
123 machine: *bodily frame*   126 more above: *more too*

As they fell out by time, by means, and place,
All given to mine ear.

   King.   But how hath she   128
Receiv'd his love?

   Pol.   What do you think of me?

   King. As of a man faithful and honorable.

   Pol. I would fain prove so. But what might you
     think,
When I had seen this hot love on the wing,—   132
As I perceiv'd it, (I must tell you that)
Before my daughter told me,—what might you,
Or my dear majesty, your queen here, think,
If I had play'd the desk or table-book,   136
Or given my heart a winking, mute and dumb,
Or look'd upon this love with idle sight?
What might you think? No, I went round to work,
And my young mistress thus I did bespeak: 140
'Lord Hamlet is a prince, out of thy star;
This must not be:' and then I prescripts gave her,
That she should lock herself from his resort,
Admit no messengers, receive no tokens.   144
Which done, she took the fruits of my advice;
And he, repelled,—a short tale to make,—
Fell into a sadness, then into a fast,
Thence to a watch, thence into a weakness,   148

127 fell out: *occurred*   means: *opportunities of access*
137 winking: *a short nap, i.e., allowed my heart to connive*
139 round: *straightforwardly*
140 bespeak: *address*
141 out of thy star: *above the position allotted thee by fortune*
142 prescripts: *positive orders*
148 watch: *state of sleeplessness*

Thence to a lightness, and by this declension
Into the madness wherein now he raves,
And all we mourn for.

King.   Do you think 'tis this?

Queen. It may be, very like.   152

Pol. Hath there been such a time,—I'd fain know that,—
That I have positively said, ' 'Tis so,'
When it prov'd otherwise?

King.   Not that I know.

Pol. Take this from this, if this be otherwise.   156
             [*Pointing to his head and shoulder.*]
If circumstances lead me, I will find
Where truth is hid, though it were hid indeed
Within the center.

King.   How may we try it further?

Pol. You know sometimes he walks four hours to-
     gether   160
Here in the lobby.

Queen.   So he does indeed.

Pol. At such a time I'll loose my daughter to him.
Be you and I behind an arras then.
Mark the encounter; if he love her not,   164
And be not from his reason fallen thereon,
Let me be no assistant for a state,
But keep a farm and carters.

King.   We will try it.

Enter Hamlet reading on a book.

149 lightness: *lightheadedness*   declension: *downward course*
159 center: *middle point of the earth*
163 arras: *hanging tapestry*

Queen. But look, where sadly the poor wretch comes
    reading.   168
Pol. Away! I do beseech you, both away.
I'll board him presently. O, give me leave.

                    Exeunt King and Queen.

How does my good Lord Hamlet?
    Ham. Well, God-a-mercy.   172
    Pol. Do you know me, my lord?
    Ham. Excellent well. You are a fishmonger.
    Pol. Not I, my lord.
    Ham. Then I would you were so honest a man.   176
    Pol. Honest, my lord?
    Ham. Ay, sir; to be honest, as this world goes, is
to be one man picked out of ten thousand.
    Pol. That's very true, my lord.   180
    Ham. For if the sun breed maggots in a dead dog,
being a god kissing carrion,—Have you a daughter?
    Pol. I have, my lord.
    Ham. Let her not walk i' the sun. Conception is a
blessing, but as your daughter may conceive, friend,
look to 't.   186
    Pol. [*Aside.*] How say you by that? Still harping
on my daughter. Yet he knew me not at first; 'a said
I was a fishmonger. 'A is far gone; and truly in my
youth I suffered much extremity for love, very near
this. I'll speak to him again. What do you read, my
lord?   192
    Ham. Words, words, words.
    Pol. What is the matter, my lord?

170 board: *accost*   presently: *immediately*
174 fishmonger; *cf. n.*
182 god kissing; *cf. n.*
                    194 matter: *substance*

Ham. Between who?

Pol. I mean the matter that you read, my lord.   196

Ham. Slanders, sir: for the satirical rogue says here that old men have grey beards, that their faces are wrinkled, their eyes purging thick amber and plum-tree gum, and that they have a plentiful lack of wit, together with most weak hams. All which, sir, though I most powerfully and potently believe, yet I hold it not honesty to have it thus set down; for yourself, sir, shall grow old as I am, if, like a crab, you could go backward.   205

Pol. [*Aside.*] Though this be madness, yet there is method in 't. Will you walk out of the air, my lord?

Ham. Into my grave?   208

Pol. Indeed, that 's out of the air. [*Aside.*] How pregnant sometimes his replies are! a happiness that often madness hits on, which reason and sanity could not so prosperously be delivered of. I will leave him and suddenly contrive the means of meeting between him and my daughter. My honorable lord, I will most humbly take my leave of you.   215

Ham. You cannot take from me anything that I will more willingly part withal,—except my life, except my life, except my life.

Pol. Fare you well, my lord.   [*Going.*]

Ham. These tedious old fools!

Enter Guildenstern and Rosencrantz.

Pol. You go to seek the Lord Hamlet? There he is.

195 Between who?; *cf. n.*   199 purging: *discharging*
199–200 amber . . . gum; *cf. n.*   203 honesty: *decency*
210 pregnant: *full of meaning*   happiness: *appropriateness*
212 prosperously: *successfully*   217 withal: *with*

Ros. [*To Polonius.*] God save you, sir!   222
                                                        [*Exit Polonius.*]

   Guil. My honored lord!

   Ros. My most dear lord!

   Ham. My excellent good friends! How dost thou, Guildenstern? Ah, Rosencrantz! Good lads, how do you both?   227

   Ros. As the indifferent children of the earth.

   Guil. Happy in that we are not over happy; on Fortune's cap we are not the very button.

   Ham. Nor the soles of her shoe?   231

   Ros. Neither, my lord.

   Ham. Then you live about her waist, or in the middle of her favors?

   Guil. Faith, her privates we.   235

   Ham. In the secret parts of Fortune? O, most true; she is a strumpet. What news?

   Ros. None, my lord, but that the world's grown honest.   239

   Ham. Then is doomsday near; but your news is not true. ⟨Let me question more in particular. What have you, my good friends, deserved at the hands of Fortune, that she sends you to prison hither?

   Guil. Prison, my lord!   244

   Ham. Denmark's a prison.

   Ros. Then is the world one.

   Ham. A goodly one; in which there are many confines, wards, and dungeons, Denmark being one o' the worst.   249

228 indifferent: *ordinary, average*
229–230 on . . . button; *cf. n.*   237 strumpet; *cf. n.*
241–271 Let me . . . attended; *not in Quarto*

Ros. We think not so, my lord.

Ham. Why, then, 'tis none to you; for there is nothing either good or bad but thinking makes it so. To me it is a prison.   253

Ros. Why, then your ambition makes it one; 'tis too narrow for your mind.

Ham. O God, I could be bounded in a nutshell, and count myself a king of infinite space, were it not that I have bad dreams.   258

Guil. Which dreams, indeed, are ambition, for the very substance of the ambitious is merely the shadow of a dream.   261

Ham. A dream itself is but a shadow.

Ros. Truly, and I hold ambition of so airy and light a quality that it is but a shadow's shadow.   264

Ham. Then are our beggars bodies, and our monarchs and outstretched heroes the beggars' shadows. Shall we to the court? for, by my fay, I cannot reason.

Both. We'll wait upon you.   268

Ham. No such matter. I will not sort you with the rest of my servants, for, to speak to you like an honest man, I am most dreadfully attended.⟩ But, in the beaten way of friendship, what make you at Elsinore?

Ros. To visit you, my lord; no other occasion.   274

Ham. Beggar that I am, I am even poor in thanks, but I thank you: and sure, dear friends, my thanks are too dear a halfpenny. Were you not sent for?

264 quality: *nature*   265 beggars bodies; *cf. n.*
266 outstretched: *strutting*   267 fay: *faith*   reason: *argue*
268 wait upon: *attend*   269 sort: *class*
272 beaten: *well-worn, reliable*
277 too dear a halfpenny; *cf. n.*

Is it your own inclining? Is it a free visitation? Come,
come, deal justly with me: come, come; nay, speak.

Guil. What should we say, my lord? 280

Ham. Why anything, but to the purpose. You
were sent for; and there is a kind of confession in
your looks which your modesties have not craft
enough to color. I know the good king and queen
have sent for you. 285

Ros. To what end, my lord?

Ham. That you must teach me. But let me conjure
you, by the rights of our fellowship, by the consonancy of our youth, by the obligation of our ever-
preserved love, and by what more dear a better
proposer could charge you withal, be even and direct
with me, whether you were sent for or no. 292

Ros. [*Aside to Guildenstern.*] What say you?

Ham. Nay, then, I have an eye of you. If you love
me, hold not off.

Guil. My lord, we were sent for. 296

Ham. I will tell you why; so shall my anticipation
prevent your discovery, and your secrecy to the king
and queen moult no feather. I have of late,—but
wherefore I know not,—lost all my mirth, forgone all
custom of exercises; and indeed it goes so heavily
with my disposition that this goodly frame, the earth,
seems to me a sterile promontory; this most excellent

278 free: *voluntary*   284 color: *disguise*
287 conjure: *adjure*   288–289 consonancy: *harmony*
290–291 better proposer: *more skillful exhorter*
291 even: *straightforward*
294 have an eye of you: *have an eye upon you*
298 prevent: *precede*   discovery: *disclosure*

canopy, the air, look you, this brave o'erhanging
firmament, this majestical roof fretted with golden
fire, why, it appeareth nothing to me but a foul and
pestilent congregation of vapors. What a piece of
work is a man! How noble in reason! how infinite in
faculties! in form and moving how express and admirable! in action how like an angel! in apprehension
how like a god! the beauty of the world, the para-
gon of animals. And yet to me what is this quintessence of dust? Man delights not me; no, nor woman
neither, though by your smiling you seem to say so.

Ros. My lord, there was no such stuff in my
thoughts.   316

Ham. Why did ye laugh, then, when I said 'man
delights not me'? Players first mentioned

Ros. To think, my lord, if you delight not in man,
what lenten entertainment the players shall receive
from you. We coted them on the way; and hither
are they coming, to offer you service.   322

Ham. He that plays the king shall be welcome,
his majesty shall have tribute of me; the adventurous
knight shall use his foil and target; the lover shall
not sigh gratis; the humorous man shall end his part
in peace; ⟨the clown shall make those laugh whose

304 brave: *splendid*   305 fretted: *adorned*
309 faculties: *powers*   express: *well-modelled*
310 apprehension: *understanding*
312–313 quintessence; *cf. n.*   315 stuff: *matter*
320 lenten: *meagre*   321 coted: *passed*
325 foil and target: *sword and shield*
326 humorous man: *actor of whimsical characters; cf. n.*
327–328 the clown . . . sere; *not in Quarto*

lungs are tickle o' the sere;) and the lady shall say
her mind freely, or the blank verse shall halt for 't.
What players are they?   330

Ros. Even those you were wont to take delight in,
the tragedians of the city.

Ham. How chances it they travel? Their residence,
both in reputation and profit, was better both ways.

Ros. I think their inhibition comes by the means
of the late innovation.   336

Ham. Do they hold the same estimation they did
when I was in the city? Are they so followed?

Ros. No, indeed are they not.   339

⟨*Ham.* How comes it? Do they grow rusty?

Ros. Nay, their endeavor keeps in the wonted
pace: but there is, sir, an aery of children, little
eyases, that cry out on the top of question, and are
most tyrannically clapped for 't. These are now the
fashion, and so berattle the common stages (so they
call them) that many wearing rapiers are afraid of
goose-quills, and dare scarce come thither.   347

Ham. What, are they children? who maintains

328 tickle o' the sere: *yield easily to any impulse; cf. n.*
329 halt: *limp*   333 residence: *remaining at headquarters*
335 inhibition: *hindrance*   336 innovation; *cf. n.*
337 estimation: *reputation*   338 the city; *cf. n.*
340–365 How comes it . . . his load too; *not in Quarto*
342 aery: *nest; cf. n.*
343 eyases: *young hawks*   **cry . . . question:** *deal pungently
with the latest gossip*
344 tyrannically: *outrageously*
345 berattle: *decry*   common stages; *cf. n.*
346 many wearing rapiers: *many men of quality*
346–347 afraid of goose-quills: *afraid of being satirized; cf. n.*

[handwritten marginalia: expressing his dislike of these performances]

'em? how are they escoted? Will they pursue the
quality no longer than they can sing? Will they not
say afterwards, if they should grow themselves to
common players (as it is most like, if their means
are no better) their writers do them wrong to make
them exclaim against their own succession?   354

Ros. Faith, there has been much to-do on both
sides, and the nation holds it no sin to tarre them to
controversy. There was for a while no money bid for
argument, unless the poet and the player went to
cuffs in the question.   359

Ham. Is 't possible?

Guil. O, there has been much throwing about of
brains.

Ham. Do the boys carry it away?

Ros. Ay, that they do, my lord—Hercules and his
load too.)   365

Ham. It is not very strange; for my uncle is king
of Denmark, and those that would make mouths at
him while my father lived give twenty, forty, fifty, a
hundred ducats apiece for his picture in little.
'Sblood, there is something in this more than natural,
if philosophy could find it out.   *A flourish.*

Guil. There are the players.   372

Ham. Gentlemen, you are welcome to Elsinore.

---

349 escoted: *maintained*   350 quality: *profession*
352 common players: *professional players*
354 succession: *future, inheritance*   356 tarre: *incite*
358 argument: *subject-matter, plot*   359 cuffs: *blows*
363 carry it away: *carry the day*
364–365 Hercules and his load; *cf. n.*   367 mouths: *grimaces*
369 in little: *in a miniature*   370 'Sblood: *God's blood*

Your hands! come then; th' appurtenance of welcome
is fashion and ceremony. Let me comply with you in
this garb, lest my extent to the players (which, I tell
you, must show fairly outwards) should more appear like entertainment than yours. You are welcome;
but my uncle-father and aunt-mother are deceived.

Guil. In what, my dear lord?   380

Ham. I am but mad north-north-west. When the
wind is southerly, I know a hawk from a handsaw.

Enter Polonius.

Pol. Well be with you, gentlemen!   383

Ham. Hark you, Guildenstern, and you too! at
each ear a hearer. That great baby you see there is
not yet out of his swaddling-clouts.

Ros. Happily he is the second time come to them,
for they say an old man is twice a child.   388

Ham. I will prophesy he comes to tell me of the
players; mark it.—You say right, sir; o' Monday morning. 'Twas then indeed.

Pol. My lord, I have news to tell you.

Ham. My lord, I have news to tell you. When
Roscius was an actor in Rome,—   394

Pol. The actors are come hither, my lord.

Ham. Buzz, buzz!

Pol. Upon my honor,—   397

374 appurtenance: *proper accompaniment*
375 comply: *observe the formalities of courtesy*
376 garb: *manner*   extent: *showing of kindness*
378 entertainment: *hospitality*   382 handsaw; *cf. n.*
386 swaddling-clouts: *bandages in which newborn children were
    wrapped*
394 Roscius; *cf. n.*
396 Buzz, buzz: *an exclamation of contempt*

Ham. Then came each actor on his ass,—

Pol. The best actors in the world, either for tragedy, comedy, history, pastoral, pastoral-comical, historical-pastoral, ⟨tragical-historical, tragical-comical-
historical-pastoral,⟩ scene individable, or poem
unlimited: Seneca cannot be too heavy, nor Plautus
too light. For the law of writ and the liberty, these
are the only men.   405
    Ham. O Jephthah, judge of Israel, what a treasure
hadst thou!
    Pol. What a treasure had he, my lord?
    Ham. Why,   409

One fair daughter and no more,
The which he loved passing well.

    Pol. [*Aside.*] Still on my daughter.   412
    Ham. Am I not i' the right, old Jephthah?
    Pol. If you call me Jephthah, my lord, I have a
daughter that I love passing well.
    Ham. Nay, that follows not.   416
    Pol. What follows, then, my lord?
    Ham. Why,

As by lot, God wot.

And then, you know,   420

It came to pass, as most like it was,—

402 scene individable; *cf. n.*
402–403 poem unlimited; *cf. n.*   Seneca; *cf. n.*   Plautus;
    cf. n.
404 law of writ and the liberty; *cf. n.*
406 Jephthah: *hero of an old ballad quoted below*
421 'as most like it was': *as was most probable*

The first row of the pious chanson will show you
more, for look where my abridgment comes.   423

Enter four or five Players.

You are welcome, masters; welcome, all. I am glad to
see thee well. Welcome, good friends. O, my old
friend? Why thy face is valanced since I saw thee
last: com'st thou to beard me in Denmark? What,
my young lady and mistress! By 'r lady, your lady-
ship is nearer to heaven than when I saw you last by
the altitude of a chopine. Pray God, your voice, like a
piece of uncurrent gold, be not cracked within the
ring. Masters, you are all welcome. We'll e'en to 't
like French falconers, fly at anything we see: we'll
have a speech straight. Come, give us a taste of
your quality; come, a passionate speech.   435

Player. What speech, my good lord?

Ham. I heard thee speak me a speech once, but it
was never acted; or, if it was, not above once; for the
play, I remember, pleased not the million; 'twas
caviary to the general: but it was (as I received it,
and others, whose judgments in such matters cried in
the top of mine) an excellent play, well digested in

422 row: *stanza, or column of print*   chanson: *song*
423 abridgment: *something to cut short my talk*
426 valanced: *'curtained,' with a beard*
430 chopine: *a Venetian raised shoe worn by women*
431 uncurrent: *not passable as lawful coinage*   cracked . . .
    ring; *cf. n.*
434 straight: *immediately*
440 caviary . . . general; *cf. n.*
441–442 cried in the top of: *spoke with a louder voice of author-
        ity than*   digested: *arranged*

the scenes, set down with as much modesty as cunning. I remember one said there were no sallets in
the lines to make the matter savory, nor no matter in
the phrase that might indict the author of affection;
but called it an honest method, «as wholesome as
sweet, and by very much more handsome than fine.»
One speech in 't I chiefly loved; 'twas Æneas' tale to
Dido; and thereabout of it especially, where he speaks
of Priam's slaughter. If it live in your memory, begin
at this line: let me see, let me see:—   452

The rugged Pyrrhus, like th' Hyrcanian beast,—

'Tis not so. It begins with Pyrrhus:—

The rugged Pyrrhus, he, whose sable arms,
Black as his purpose, did the night resemble   456
When he lay couched in the ominous horse,
Hath now this dread and black complexion smear'd
With heraldry more dismal. Head to foot
Now is he total gules, horridly trick'd   460
With blood of fathers, mothers, daughters, sons,
Bak'd and impasted with the parching streets,
That lend a tyrannous and a damned light
To their lords' murther. Roasted in wrath and fire,   464
And thus o'er-sized with coagulate gore,

443 modesty: *moderation*   cunning: *skill in technique*
444–445 sallets . . . savory; *cf. n.*
446 indict: *convict*   affection: *affectation*
447–448 as wholesome . . . fine; *not in Folio*
448 handsome; *cf. n.*   fine: *elaborately fashioned*
449–450 Æneas' tale to Dido; *cf. n.*
453 Hyrcanian; *cf. n.*   457 ominous horse; *cf. n.*
460 total gules: *red all over*   trick'd: *spotted*
462 impasted: *made into a crust*
465 o'er-sized: *covered with something like size, a kind of glue*

With eyes like carbuncles, the hellish Pyrrhus
Old grandsire Priam seeks.

«So proceed you.»   468
    Pol. 'Fore God, my lord, well spoken! with good
    accent and good discretion.

   Player.   Anon, he finds him
Striking too short at Greeks; his antique sword,
Rebellious to his arm, lies where it falls,   472
Repugnant to command. Unequal match'd,
Pyrrhus at Priam drives, in rage strikes wide;
But with the whiff and wind of his fell sword
Th' unnerved father falls. ⟨Then senseless Ilium,⟩   476
Seeming to feel this blow, with flaming top
Stoops to his base, and with a hideous crash
Takes prisoner Pyrrhus' ear: for lo, his sword,
Which was declining on the milky head   480
Of reverend Priam, seem'd i' th' air to stick.
So as a painted tyrant Pyrrhus stood,
And like a neutral to his will and matter,
Did nothing.   484
But as we often see against some storm
A silence in the heavens, the rack stand still,
The bold winds speechless and the orb below
As hush as death, anon the dreadful thunder   488
Doth rend the region; so, after Pyrrhus' pause,
A roused vengeance sets him new a-work;
And never did the Cyclops' hammers fall
On Mars's armor, forg'd for proof eterne,   492

466 carbuncles: *glittering red stones, rubies*
473 Repugnant to: *resisting*   475 fell: *cruel*
476 senseless: *incapable of feeling*
482 painted tyrant: *picture of an oppressor*
483 a neutral: *one indifferent*   matter: *task*
485 against: *just before*   486 rack: *mass of cloud*
488 anon: *presently*   489 region: *the air*
491 Cyclops': *Vulcan's workmen's*
492 proof eterne: *eternal impenetrability*

With less remorse than Pyrrhus' bleeding sword
Now falls on Priam.
Out, out, thou strumpet Fortune! All you gods,
In general synod take away her power,   496
Break all the spokes and fellies from her wheel,
And bowl the round nave down the hill of heaven
As low as to the fiends!

    Pol. This is too long.   500
    Ham. It shall to the barber's, with your beard.
Prithee, say on: he's for a jig or a tale of bawdry, or
he sleeps. Say on; come to Hecuba.

Player. But who, O who, had seen the mobled queen—

    Ham. 'The mobled queen'?   505
    Pol. That's good; ⟨'mobled queen' is good.⟩

Player. Run barefoot up and down, threat'ning the
     flames   507
With bisson rheum,—a clout upon that head
Where late the diadem stood, and for a robe,
About her lank and all o'er-teemed loins,
A blanket, in the alarm of fear caught up,—   511
Who this had seen, with tongue in venom steep'd,
'Gainst Fortune's state would treason have pronounc'd.
But if the gods themselves did see her then,
When she saw Pyrrhus make malicious sport
In mincing with his sword her husband's limbs,   516
The instant burst of clamor that she made

496 synod: *assembly*
497 fellies: *the pieces of wood of which the circumference is made*
498 nave: *hub*
502 jig: *lively dance, often accompanied by coarse comic verses or dialogue*
504 mobled: *muffled*
508 bisson rheum: *blinding tears*   clout: *piece of cloth*
510 o'er-teemed: *exhausted by excessive child-bearing*

(Unless things mortal move them not at all)
Would have made milch the burning eyes of heaven   519
And passion in the gods.

Pol. Look! wh'er he has not turned his color and
has tears in 's eyes. Prithee, no more.   522

Ham. 'Tis well. I'll have thee speak out the rest of
this soon. Good my lord, will you see the players well
bestowed? Do you hear, let them be well used, for
they are the abstract and brief chronicles of the time.
After your death you were better have a bad epitaph
than their ill report while you live.

Pol. My lord, I will use them according to their
desert.   530

Ham. God's bodkin, man, much better! Use every
man after his desert, and who shall 'scape whipping?
Use them after your own honor and dignity: the
less they deserve, the more merit is in your bounty.
Take them in.   535

Pol. Come, sirs.

Ham. Follow him, friends: we'll hear a play to-
morrow. *Exit Polonius* [*with all the Players but the
First.*] Dost thou hear me, old friend; can you play
the Murther of Gonzago?   540

Player. Ay, my lord.

Ham. We'll ha 't to-morrow night. You could, for
a need, study a speech of some dozen or sixteen lines,
which I would set down and insert in 't, could you
not?

519 milch: *milky, moist*   521 turned . . . color: *grown pale*
525 bestowed: *lodged*   526 abstract: *summary*
531 God's bodkin; *cf. n.*   540 Gonzago; *cf. n.*
542–543 for a need: *in case of necessity*   some dozen or six-
        teen lines; *cf. n.*

Hamlet curses himself for not displaying his emotions as the actor has done with a character who means nothing to him

Player. Ay, my lord.   546

Ham. Very well. Follow that lord, and look you mock him not. [*Exit Player. To Rosencrantz and Guildenstern.*] My good friends, I'll leave you till night. You are welcome to Elsinore.   550

Ros. Good my lord!

Ham. Ay, so! Goodbye to you!

         Exeunt [*Ros. and Guil.*]. *Manet Hamlet.*
         Now I am alone.

O what a rogue and peasant slave am I!

Is it not monstrous that this player here,   554

But in a fiction, in a dream of passion,

Could force his soul so to his own conceit

That from her working all the visage wann'd,

Tears in his eyes, distraction in 's aspect,   558

A broken voice, and his whole function suiting

With forms to his conceit? and all for nothing!

For Hecuba?

What's Hecuba to him or he to Hecuba,   562

That he should weep for her? What would he do

Had he the motive and the cue for passion

That I have? He would drown the stage with tears,

And cleave the general ear with horrid speech,   566

Make mad the guilty and appal the free,

Confound the ignorant, and amaze indeed

The very faculties of eyes and ears.

Yet I,   570

552 s.d. Manet: *remains on the stage*
553 peasant: *base*   556 conceit: *imagination*
557 wann'd: *grew pale*
559 function: *action of the body*   suiting: *fitting*
560 forms: *bodily expression*   564 cue; *cf. n.*
566 horrid: *horrible*   567 free: *free from offence, guiltless*

A dull and muddy-mettled rascal, peak,
Like John-a-dreams, unpregnant of my cause,
And can say nothing; no, not for a king,
Upon whose property and most dear life   574
A damn'd defeat was made. Am I a coward?
Who calls me villain? breaks my pate across?
Plucks off my beard and blows it in my face?   577
Tweaks me by the nose? gives me the lie i' th' throat,
As deep as to the lungs? Who does me this, ha?
'Swounds, I should take it, for it cannot be
But I am pigeon-liver'd, and lack gall
To make oppression bitter, or ere this   582
I should ha' fatted all the region kites
With this slave's offal. Bloody, bawdy villain!
Remorseless, treacherous, lecherous, kindless villain!   585
⟨O! vengeance!⟩
Why, what an ass am I! This is most brave
That I, the son of a dear murthered,
Prompted to my revenge by heaven and hell,
Must like a whore unpack my heart with words,   590
And fall a-cursing like a very drab,
A scullion! Fie upon it, foh!
About, my brains!—Hum,—. I have heard,

571 muddy-mettled: *dull-spirited*   peak: *mope about*
572 John-a-dreams: *dreamy fellow; cf. n.*   unpregnant of: *not quickened by*
574 property; *cf. n.*   575 defeat: *destruction*
580 'Swounds: *God's wounds*
581 But: *but that*   pigeon-liver'd: *meek; cf. n.*
582 make oppression bitter: *make me feel the bitterness of oppression*
583 region kites: *vultures of the air*   585 kindless: *unnatural*
588 murthered; *cf. n.* 592 scullion: *the lowest household servant*
593 About, my brains: *let me think less wildly*

That guilty creatures sitting at a play   594
Have by the very cunning of the scene
Been struck so to the soul that presently
They have proclaim'd their malefactions;
For murther, though it have no tongue, will speak   598
With most miraculous organ. I'll have these players
Play something like the murther of my father
Before mine uncle. I'll observe his looks,
I'll tent him to the quick. If 'a do blench,   602
I know my course. The spirit that I have seen
May be a de'il, and the de'il hath power
T' assume a pleasing shape;—yea, and perhaps
Out of my weakness and my melancholy   606
(As he is very potent with such spirits)
Abuses me to damn me. I'll have grounds
More relative than this. The play's the thing   609
Wherein I'll catch the conscience of the king.   *Exit.*

602 tent: *probe*   blench: *start aside*
604 de'il: *devil*   609 relative: *relevant, to the purpose*

plans to have players reinact
the murder of king to see
if it will bring about reaction
from king.

[ACT THIRD

SCENE FIRST.

A Room in the Castle]

Enter King, Queen, Polonius, Ophelia, Rosencrantz, Guildenstern, and Lords.

King. And can you by no drift of conference
Get from him why he puts on this confusion,
Grating so harshly all his days of quiet
With turbulent and dangerous lunacy?   4
Ros. He does confess he feels himself distracted,
But from what cause 'a will by no means speak.
Guil. Nor do we find him forward to be sounded,
But with a crafty madness keeps aloof,   8
When we would bring him on to some confession
Of his true state.
Queen.   Did he receive you well?
Ros. Most like a gentleman.
Guil. But with much forcing of his disposition.   12
Ros. Niggard of question, but of our demands
Most free in his reply.
Queen.   Did you assay him
To any pastime?

1 drift of conference: *turn of the conversation*
2 confusion: *distraction*   3 Grating: *harassing*
7 forward: *ready, disposed*
12 forcing of his disposition: *constraint*
13 Niggard of question: *sparing of conversation; cf. n.*
14 assay: *tempt*

Ros. Madam, it so fell out that certain players   16
We o'er-raught on the way; of these we told him,
And there did seem in him a kind of joy
To hear of it. They are about the court,
And, as I think, they have already order   20
This night to play before him.

Pol.   'Tis most true;
And he beseech'd me to entreat your majesties
To hear and see the matter.

King. With all my heart; and it doth much content
    me   24
To hear him so inclin'd.
Good gentlemen, give him a further edge,
And drive his purpose into these delights.

Ros. We shall, my lord.

                    Exeunt Ros. and Guil.
King.   Sweet Gertrude, leave us too;
For we have closely sent for Hamlet hither,   29
That he, as 'twere by accident, may here
Affront Ophelia.
Her father and myself (lawful espials)   32
Will so bestow ourselves that, seeing unseen,
We may of their encounter frankly judge,
And gather by him, as he is behav'd,
If 't be th' affliction of his love or no   36
That thus he suffers for.

Queen.   I shall obey you.
And for your part, Ophelia, I do wish
That your good beauties be the happy cause

17 o'er-raught: *overtook*   26 edge: *incitement*
29 closely: *privately*   31 Affront: *meet*
32 espials: *spies*   34 frankly: *freely*

Of Hamlet's wildness; so shall I hope your virtues   40
Will bring him to his wonted way again,
To both your honors.

    Oph.   Madam, I wish it may.

                                [Exit Queen.]

    Pol. Ophelia, walk you here. Gracious, so please you,
We will bestow ourselves. [*To Ophelia.*] Read on this
        book,   44
That show of such an exercise may color
Your loneliness. We are oft to blame in this;
'Tis too much prov'd that with devotion's visage
And pious action we do sugar o'er   48
The devil himself.

    King. [*Aside.*]   O 'tis too true!
How smart a lash that speech doth give my conscience!
The harlot's cheek, beautied with plastering art,
Is not more ugly to the thing that helps it   52
Than is my deed to my most painted word.
O heavy burthen!

    Pol. I hear him coming; let's withdraw, my lord.

                     Exeunt [King and Polonius].

                  Enter Hamlet.

    Ham. To be, or not to be, that is the question: 56
Whether 'tis nobler in the mind to suffer
The slings and arrows of outrageous fortune,

40 wildness: *madness*
43 Gracious . . . you: *if it please your Grace*
45 exercise: *religious devotion*
47 too much prov'd: *found by too frequent experience*
52 to: *in comparison with*   the thing: *the beautifying cosmetic*
56 *Cf. n.*

Or to take arms against a sea of troubles
And by opposing end them. To die: to sleep.   60
No more; and by a sleep to say we end
The heart-ache and the thousand natural shocks
That flesh is heir to: 'tis a consummation
Devoutly to be wish'd. To die: to sleep.   64
To sleep? perchance to dream. Ay, there's the rub;
For in that sleep of death what dreams may come,
When we have shuffled off this mortal coil,
Must give us pause. There's the respect   68
That makes calamity of so long life;
For who would bear the whips and scorns of time,
Th' oppressor's wrong, the proud man's contumely,
The pangs of dispriz'd love, the law's delay,   72
The insolence of office, and the spurns
That patient merit of th' unworthy takes,
When he himself might his quietus make
With a bare bodkin? Who would fardels bear,   76
To grunt and sweat under a weary life,
But that the dread of something after death,
The undiscover'd country from whose bourn
No traveller returns, puzzles the will,   80
And makes us rather bear those ills we have
Than fly to others that we know not of?

59 take . . . troubles; *cf. n.*   65 rub: *obstacle*
67 shuffled off: *sloughed off*   mortal coil: *turmoil of mortal life*
68 give us pause: *cause us to hesitate*   respect: *consideration*
69 *Cf. n.*   70 For who would bear, etc.; *cf. n.*
72 dispriz'd: *held in contempt*
73 office: *people holding official position*   spurns: *insults*
75 quietus: *release from life*
76 bare bodkin; *cf. n.*   fardels: *burdens*
79 bourn: *boundary*
80 No traveller returns; *cf. n.*   puzzles: *frustrates*

Thus conscience does make cowards of us all,
And thus the native hue of resolution   84
Is sicklied o'er with the pale cast of thought,
And enterprises of great pitch and moment
With this regard their currents turn awry,
And lose the name of action.—Soft you now!   88
The fair Ophelia! Nymph, in thy orisons
Be all my sins remember'd.

    Oph.   Good my lord,
How does your honor for this many a day?

    Ham. I humbly thank you; well, well, well.   92

    Oph. My lord, I have remembrances of yours,
That I have longed long to re-deliver;
I pray you now, receive them.

    Ham.   No, not I.
I never gave you aught.   96

    Oph. My honor'd lord, you know right well you did;
And, with them, words of so sweet breath compos'd
As made the things more rich. Their perfume lost,
Take these again, for to the noble mind   100
Rich gifts wax poor when givers prove unkind.
There, my lord.

       Ham. Ha, ha! are you honest?

       Oph. My lord!   104

       Ham. Are you fair?

       Oph. What means your lordship?

83 conscience: *the ability to think*
84 native hue: *healthy complexion*   85 cast: *tinge*
86 pitch and moment: *elevation and importance*
87 regard: *consideration*   currents: *courses*
89 orisons: *prayers*
91 for this many a day: *all this long time*
103 honest: *sincere*

Ham. That if you be honest and fair, your honesty should admit no discourse to your beauty.   108

Oph. Could beauty, my lord, have better commerce than with honesty?

Ham. Ay, truly; for the power of beauty will sooner transform honesty from what it is to a bawd than the force of honesty can translate beauty into his likeness. This was sometime a paradox, but now the time gives it proof. I did love you once.   115

Oph. Indeed, my lord, you made me believe so.

Ham. You should not have believed me, for virtue cannot so inoculate our old stock but we shall relish of it. I loved you not.

Oph. I was the more deceived.   120

Ham. Get thee to a nunnery. Why wouldst thou be a breeder of sinners? I am myself indifferent honest, but yet I could accuse me of such things that it were better my mother had not borne me. I am very proud, revengeful, ambitious, with more of-fences at my beck than I have thoughts to put them in, imagination to give them shape, or time to act them in. What should such fellows as I do crawling between earth and heaven? We are arrant knaves all; believe none of us. Go thy ways to a nunnery.— Where's your father?   131

Oph. At home, my lord.

Ham. Let the doors be shut upon him, that he

107 honest: *here in special sense of 'chaste'*
109 commerce: *intercourse*
114 paradox: *absurdity*   115 time: *present age*
118 inoculate: *engraft; cf. n.*   relish: *taste*
121 nunnery; *cf. n.*   122 indifferent: *tolerably*
126 beck: *command*   131 Where's your father; *cf. n.*

may play the fool nowhere but in 's own house.
Farewell.

Oph. O help him, you sweet heavens!   136

Ham. If thou dost marry, I'll give thee this plague
for thy dowry: be thou as chaste as ice, as pure as
snow, thou shalt not escape calumny. Get thee to a
nunnery. Go; farewell. Or if thou wilt needs marry,
marry a fool; for wise men know well enough what
monsters you make of them. To a nunnery, go, and
quickly too. Farewell.   143

Oph. O heavenly powers, restore him!

Ham. I have heard of your paintings too, well
enough. God hath given you one face, and you make
yourselves another. You jig, you amble, and you lisp.
You nickname God's creatures, and make your wantonness your ignorance. Go to, I'll no more on 't; it
hath made me mad. I say, we will have no mo
marriage. Those that are married already, all but
one, shall live; the rest shall keep as they are. To a
nunnery, go.   *Exit Hamlet.*

Oph. O what a noble mind is here o'erthrown!   154
The courtier's, soldier's, scholar's, eye, tongue, sword;
Th' expectancy and rose of the fair state,
The glass of fashion and the mould of form,
Th' observ'd of all observers, quite, quite down!
And I, of ladies most deject and wretched,   159
That suck'd the honey of his music vows,

145 your paintings: *i.e., that women paint their faces*
148 nickname: *travesty; cf. n.*   make your wantonness your
    ignorance: *affect ignorance as a mask for wantonness*
149 on 't: *of it*   150 mo: *more*
156 expectancy and rose: *hope and pride*
157 glass: *mirror*   mould: *model*

Now see that noble and most sovereign reason,
Like sweet bells jangled, out of tune and harsh;
That unmatch'd form and feature of blown youth   163
Blasted with ecstasy. O woe is me,
T' have seen what I have seen, see what I see!

Obviously not Ophelias love that B huses Hamlet
To be onstate she Claudius will send him to England

Enter King and Polonius.

King. Love! his affections do not that way tend;
Nor what he spake, though it lack'd form a little,   167
Was not like madness. There's something in his soul
O'er which his melancholy sits on brood,
And I do doubt, the hatch and the disclose
Will be some danger; which for to prevent,   171
I have in quick determination
Thus set it down: he shall with speed to England
For the demand of our neglected tribute.
Haply the seas and countries different   175
With variable objects shall expel
This something-settled matter in his heart,
Whereon his brain's still-beating puts him thus
From fashion of himself. What think you on 't?

Pol. It shall do well: but yet do I believe   180
The origin and commencement of his grief
Sprung from neglected love. How now, Ophelia!
You need not tell us what Lord Hamlet said;

161 sovereign: *supreme*
163 feature: *proportion of the whole body* ('stature' in Q 2)
    blown: *full-blown*
164 Blasted: *withered*
170 disclose: *opening of the shell, coming to life*
176 variable objects: *variety of interests*
177 something-settled: *somewhat settled*
178 still-beating: *constant hammering*
179 fashion of himself: *his ordinary manner*

We heard it all. My lord, do as you please;   184
But if you hold it fit, after the play
Let his queen mother all alone entreat him
To show his grief. Let her be round with him,   187
And I'll be plac'd (so please you) in the ear
Of all their conference. If she find him not,
To England send him, or confine him where
Your wisdom best shall think.

    King.   It shall be so.   191
Madness in great ones must not unwatch'd go.   *Exeunt.*

[SCENE SECOND.

A Hall in the Castle]

Enter Hamlet and three of the Players.

  Ham. Speak the speech, I pray you, as I pronounced it to you, trippingly on the tongue; but if
you mouth it, as many of our players do, I had as
lief the town-crier spoke my lines. Nor do not saw the
air too much with your hand, thus; but use all gently,
for in the very torrent, tempest, and (as I may say)
whirlwind of your passion, you must acquire and
beget a temperance that may give it smoothness.
O it offends me to the soul to hear a robustious periwig-pated fellow tear a passion to tatters, to very rags,

---

189 find: *see through, interpret*
2 trippingly: *rapidly, but with neat articulation*
3 mouth: *speak loudly with false emphasis and indistinctness*
7 acquire and beget: *achieve yourself and inspire in your hearers*
8 temperance: *moderation*
9 robustious: *boisterous*   periwig-pated: *wearing a wig*

to split the ears of the groundlings, who for the most part are capable of nothing but inexplicable dumb-shows and noise. I would have such a fellow whipped for o'er-doing Termagant. It out-herods Herod: pray you, avoid it. 15

Player. I warrant your honor.

Ham. Be not too tame neither, but let your own discretion be your tutor. Suit the action to the word, the word to the action, with this special observance, that you o'erstep not the modesty of nature; for anything so overdone is from the purpose of playing, whose end, both at the first and now, was and is to hold, as 'twere, the mirror up to nature, to show virtue her own feature, scorn her own image, and the very age and body of the time his form and pressure. Now this overdone, or come tardy off, though it makes the unskilful laugh, cannot but make the judicious grieve, the censure of the which one must in your allowance o'erweigh a whole theater of others. O there be players that I have seen play and heard others praise, and that highly (not to speak it profanely) that, neither having the accent of Christians nor the gait of Christian, pagan, nor man, have so strutted and bellowed that I have thought some of

11 groundlings; *cf. n.*
12 capable of: *able to enjoy*   inexplicable dumb-shows; *cf. n.*
14 Termagant; *cf. n.*   out-herods Herod; *cf. n.*
21 from: *alien to*
25 very age . . . pressure: *even the contemporary and actual quality of the present time*
25 pressure: *impressed character, stamp*
26 come tardy off: *inadequately done*
28 the which one: *one of whom*
29 allowance: *estimation*

nature's journeymen had made men and not made
them well, they imitated humanity so abominably.

Player. I hope we have reformed that indifferently
with us, sir.   38

Ham. O reform it altogether. And let those that
play your clowns speak no more than is set down for
them; for there be of them that will themselves
laugh, to set on some quantity of barren spectators
to laugh too, though in the mean time some necessary question of the play be then to be considered.
That's villainous, and shows a most pitiful ambition
in the fool that uses it. Go, make you ready.

Exeunt Players.

Enter Polonius, Guildenstern, and Rosencrantz.

How now, my lord? will the king hear this piece of work?

Pol. And the queen too, and that presently.   48

Ham. Bid the players make haste.   *Exit Polonius.*
Will you two help to hasten them?

Ros. Ay, my lord.   51

Exeunt they two.

Ham. What, ho! Horatio!

Enter Horatio.

Hor. Here, sweet lord, at your service.

Ham. Horatio, thou art e'en as just a man
As e'er my conversation cop'd withal.   55

Hor. O, my dear lord,—

Ham.   Nay, do not think I flatter;

35 journeymen: *laborers not yet masters of their trade*
41 there be of them: *there are some; cf. n.*
42 barren: *barren of wit*   54 just: *fair-minded, righteous*
55 cop'd withal: *came in contact with*

speech attempt to make character a foil

For what advancement may I hope from thee,
That no revénue hast but thy good spirits
To feed and clothe thee? Why should the poor be flat-
   ter'd?   59
No, let the candied tongue lick ábsurd pomp,
And crook the pregnant hinges of the knee
Where thrift may follow fawning. Dost thou hear?
Since my dear soul was mistress of her choice
And could of men distinguish, her election   64
Hath seal'd thee for herself; for thou hast been
As one, in suffering all, that suffers nothing,
A man that fortune's buffets and rewards   67
Hast ta'en with equal thanks; and bless'd are those
Whose blood and judgment are so well co-mingled
That they are not a pipe for fortune's finger
To sound what stop she please. Give me that man   71
That is not passion's slave, and I will wear him
In my heart's core, ay, in my heart of heart,
As I do thee. Something too much of this.
There is a play to-night before the king.   75
One scene of it comes near the circumstance
Which I have told thee of my father's death.
I prithee, when thou seest that act afoot,
Even with the very comment of thy soul   79
Observe my uncle. If his occulted guilt

60 candied: *flattering*   lick: *pay court to* (*like a dog*)   ab-
    surd: *silly*
61 pregnant hinges: *easily bent joints*   62 thrift: *profit*
64 election: *choice*   65 seal'd: *registered unchangeably*
69 blood: *passions*   co-mingled; *cf. n.*
71 stop: *a hole in wind instruments for controlling the sound;*
    cf. n.
79 very comment: *most intense observation*
80 occulted: *hidden*

Do not itself unkennel in one speech,
It is a damned ghost that we have seen,
And my imaginations are as foul   83
As Vulcan's stithy. Give him heedful note,
For I mine eyes will rivet to his face,
And after we will both our judgments join
In censure of his seeming.

    Hor.   Well, my lord,   87
If 'a steal aught the whilst this play is playing,
And 'scape detecting, I will pay the theft.

clue?   *Ham.* They are coming to the play. I must be idle.
Get you a place.   91

Enter King, Queen, Polonius, Ophelia, Rosencrantz,
    Guildenstern, and other Lords attendant, with his
    Guard carrying torches. Danish March. Sound a
    Flourish.

    King. How fares our cousin Hamlet?

    Ham. Excellent, i' faith; of the chameleon's dish.
I eat the air, promise-crammed. You cannot feed
capons so.   95

    King. I have nothing with this answer, Hamlet.
These words are not mine.

    Ham. No, nor mine now. [*To Polonius.*] My lord,
you played once i' th' university, you say?   99

    Pol. That did I, my lord, and was accounted a
good actor.

    Ham. What did you enact?   102

---

81 itself unkennel: *come to light (like a fox driven from its hole)*
    in one speech; *cf. n.*
84 Vulcan; *cf. n.*   stithy: *blacksmith's shop, forge*
87 censure: *careful criticism*   seeming: *appearance*
90 be idle: *act mad; cf. n.*   93 chameleon's dish; *cf. n.*
96 have nothing with: *can make nothing of*

Pol. I did enact Julius Cæsar. I was killed i' the Capitol. Brutus killed me.

Ham. It was a brute part of him to kill so capital a calf there. Be the players ready?   106

Ros. Ay, my lord; they stay upon your patience.

Queen. Come hither, my dear Hamlet, sit by me.

Ham. No, good mother, here's metal more attractive.   110

Pol. [*To the King.*] O ho! do you mark that?

Ham. Lady, shall I lie in your lap?

Oph. No, my lord.

⟨*Ham.* I mean, my head upon your lap?

Oph. Ay, my lord.⟩   115

Ham. Do you think I meant country matters?

Oph. I think nothing, my lord.

Ham. That's a fair thought to lie between maids' legs.

Oph. What is, my lord?   120

Ham. Nothing.

Oph. You are merry, my lord.

Ham. Who, I?

Oph. Ay, my lord.   124

Ham. O God, your only jig-maker. What should a man do but be merry? for look you how cheerfully my mother looks, and my father died within's two hours.   128

---

103 Julius Cæsar; *cf. n.*
104 Capitol; *cf. n.*   105 brute part: *stupid act*
107 stay upon: *wait for*   patience: *leisure*
114, 115   *not in Quarto*
116 country matters: *uncouth conduct; cf. n.*
125 your only jig-maker: *I am the best jig-maker there is; cf. n.*
    on II. ii. 502.   127 within's: *within this*

Oph. Nay, 'tis twice two months, my lord.

Ham. So long? Nay, then, let the de'il wear black,
for I'll have a suit of sables. O heavens! die two
months ago, and not forgotten yet? Then there's
hope a great man's memory may outlive his life half
a year; but, by 'r lady, 'a must build churches then, or
else shall 'a suffer not thinking on with the hobby-
horse, whose epitaph is, 'For, O! for, O! the hobby-
horse is forgot.'   137

Hautboys play. The dumb-show enters.

Enter a King and a Queen very lovingly, the Queen embracing
    him. She kneels and makes show of protestation unto
    him. He takes her up and declines his head upon her neck;
    lays him down upon a bank of flowers. She, seeing him
    asleep, leaves him. Anon comes in a fellow, takes off his
    crown, kisses it, and pours poison in the King's ears, and
    exit. The Queen returns, finds the King dead, and makes
    passionate action. The Poisoner, with some two or three
    Mutes, comes in again, seeming to lament with her. The
    dead body is carried away. The Poisoner wooes the Queen
    with gifts; she seems loath and unwilling awhile, but in the
    end accepts his love.   Exeunt.

Oph. What means this, my lord?

Ham. Marry, this is miching Malicho; it means
mischief.   140

129 twice two months; cf. *n.*
131 suit of sables: *suit of rich fur; cf. n.*
135 suffer not thinking on: *be forgotten*
135–136 hobby-horse: *one of the participants in the morris
    dance; cf. n.*
S. d. Hautboys: *wooden double-reed instruments of high pitch*
S. d. Mutes: *actors without speaking parts (but here all are
    mutes)*
139 miching Malicho: *skulking mischief; cf. n.*

Oph. Belike this show imports the argument of the play.

Enter Prologue.

Ham. We shall know by this fellow. The players cannot keep counsel; they'll tell all.   144

Oph. Will 'a tell us what this show meant?

Ham. Ay, or any show that you will show him. Be not you ashamed to show, he'll not shame to tell you what it means.   148

Oph. You are naught, you are naught. I'll mark the play.

Pro. For us and for our tragedy,   151
      Here stooping to your clemency,
      We beg your hearing patiently.

Ham. Is this a prologue, or the posy of a ring?   154
Oph. 'Tis brief, my lord.
Ham. As woman's love.

Enter [Player] King and Queen.

[P.] *King.* Full thirty times hath Phœbus' cart gone round   157
Neptune's salt wash and Tellus' orbed ground,
And thirty dozen moons with borrow'd sheen
About the world have times twelve thirties been,
Since love our hearts and Hymen did our hands
Unite commutual in most sacred bands.   162
[P.] *Queen.* So many journeys may the sun and moon
Make us again count o'er ere love be done!

141 imports the argument: *amounts to a synopsis*
144 counsel: *secret*   149 naught: *wanton*
152 stooping: *bowing*   154 posy: *motto*
157 cart: *chariot*   158 wash: *sea*   Tellus'; *cf. n.*
159 borrow'd sheen: *reflected light*
162 commutual: *an intensive form of 'mutual'*

But, woe is me! you are so sick of late,   165
So far from cheer and from your former state,
That I distrust you. Yet though I distrust,
Discomfort you, my lord, it nothing must;
«For women fear too much, even as they love,»
And women's fear and love hold quantity,
In neither aught, or in extremity.   171
Now what my love is, proof hath made you know;
And as my love is siz'd, my fear is so.
«Where love is great, the littlest doubts are fear;
Where little fears grow great, great love grows there.»   175
    [P.] *King.* Faith, I must leave thee, love, and shortly too.
My operant powers their functions leave to do,
And thou shalt live in this fair world behind,
Honor'd, belov'd; and haply one as kind   179
For husband shalt thou—
    [P.] *Queen.*   O confound the rest!
Such love must needs be treason in my breast.
In second husband let me be accurst;
None wed the second but who kill'd the first.   183

    Ham. [*Aside.*] That's wormwood, wormwood.

    [P.] *Queen.* The instances that second marriage move
Are base respects of thrift, but none of love;
A second time I kill my husband dead,   187
When second husband kisses me in bed.
    [P.] *King.* I do believe you think what now you speak,
But what we do determine oft we break.
Purpose is but the slave to memory,   191
Of violent birth, but poor validity;
Which now, like fruit unripe, sticks on the tree,
But fall unshaken when they mellow be.

167   I distrust you: *I have misgivings on your account*
169, 174–175 *not in Folio*   170 quantity: *proportion*
171 In . . . extremity: *nothing of either, or else an excess*
177 operant: *vital*
185 instances: *motives, inducements*   move: *suggest*
192 validity: *strength*

[handwritten marginal note:] Play queen protests against second marriage

Most necessary 'tis that we forget   195
To pay ourselves what to ourselves is debt;
What to ourselves in passion we propose,
The passion ending, doth the purpose lose.
The violence of either grief or joy   199
Their own enactures with themselves destroy;
Where joy most revels grief doth most lament,
Grief joys, joy grieves, on slender accident.
This world is not for aye, nor 'tis not strange
That even our loves should with our fortunes change,   204
For 'tis a question left us yet to prove
Whether love lead fortune or else fortune love.
The great man down, you mark his favorite flies;   207
The poor advanc'd makes friends of enemies.
And hitherto doth love on fortune tend,
For who not needs shall never lack a friend;
And who in want a hollow friend doth try   211
Directly seasons him his enemy.
But, orderly to end where I begun,
Our wills and fates do so contrary run
That our devices still are overthrown,   215
Our thoughts are ours, their ends none of our own.
So think thou wilt no second husband wed,
But die thy thoughts when thy first lord is dead.
   [P.] *Queen.* Nor earth to me give food, nor heaven
      light!   219
Sport and repose lock from me day and night!
«To desperation turn my trust and hope!
An anchor's cheer in prison be my scope!»
Each opposite that blanks the face of joy   223
Meet what I would have well, and it destroy!
Both here and hence pursue me lasting strife,
If, once a widow, ever I be wife!

---

200 enactures: *fulfilments*   211 hollow: *insincere*
216 ends: *results*   219 Nor . . . nor: *neither . . . nor*
220 Sport: *pleasure; cf. n.*
221, 222 *not in Folio*
223 opposite: *contrary thing*   222 anchor's: *anchorite's*
                                     blanks: *blanches, makes pale*

Ham. If she should break it now!   227

[*P.*] *King.* 'Tis deeply sworn. Sweet, leave me here awhile;
My spirits grow dull, and fain I would beguile
The tedious day with sleep.   *Sleeps.*
        [*P.*] *Queen*   Sleep rock thy brain;
And never come mischance between us twain!   *Exit.*

Ham. Madam, how like you this play?   232
Queen. The lady doth protest too much, me-
thinks.
Ham. O, but she'll keep her word.   235
King. Have you heard the argument? Is there no
offence in 't?
Ham. No, no, they do but jest,—poison in jest.
No offence i' th' world.
King. What do you call the play?
Ham. The Mouse-trap. Marry, how? Tropically.
This play is the image of a murther done in Vienna.
Gonzago is the duke's name; his wife, Baptista. You
shall see anon. 'Tis a knavish piece of work: but
what of that? Your majesty and we that have free
souls, it touches us not. Let the galled jade wince,
our withers are unwrung.   247

Enter [*Player as*] *Lucianus.*

This is one Lucianus, nephew to the king.
Oph. You are as good as a chorus, my lord.

241 Tropically: *figuratively; cf. n.*
242 image: *representation*   243 duke's name; *cf. n.*
246 galled jade: *horse sore from chafing*   withers: *shoulders*
247 unwrung: *not galled*
249 chorus: *in Elizabethan drama one who speaks a prologue
    summarizing the action*

Ham. I could interpret between you and your love,
if I could see the puppets dallying.   251

Oph. You are keen, my lord, you are keen.

Ham. It would cost you a groaning to take off
mine edge.   254

Oph. Still better, and worse.

Ham. So you must take your husbands. Begin,
murtherer; leave thy damnable faces, and begin.
Come; the croaking raven doth bellow for revenge.

Luc. Thoughts black, hands apt, drugs fit, and time agree-
        ing;
Confederate season, else no creature seeing.
Thou mixture rank, of midnight weeds collected,
With Hecate's ban thrice blasted, thrice infected,
Thy natural magic and dire property,   263
On wholesome life usurps immediately.

                            Pours the poison in his ears.

Ham. 'A poisons him i' the garden for his estate.
His name's Gonzago. The story is extant, and written
in very choice Italian. You shall see anon how the
murtherer gets the love of Gonzago's wife.   268

Oph. The king rises.

⟨*Ham.* What, frighted with false fire?⟩

Queen. How fares my lord?

Pol. Give o'er the play.   272

King. Give me some light! Away!

Pol. Lights, lights, lights!

                    Exeunt all but Hamlet and Horatio.

---

250 interpret; *cf. n.*   256 So . . . husbands; *cf. n.*
258 the croaking . . . revenge; *cf. n.*
260 Confederate season: *time conspiring to assist*
262 Hecate; *cf. n.*
270 *not in Quarto*   272 Give o'er: *stop*

Ham. Why, let the stricken deer go weep,
     The hart ungalled play,   276
For some must watch while some must sleep:
     Thus runs the world away.

Would not this, sir, and a forest of feathers (if the rest of my fortunes turn Turk with me) with two Provincial roses on my razed shoes, get me a fellowship in a cry of players?

     Hor. Half a share.

     Ham. A whole one, I.   284

     For thou dost know, O Damon dear,
         This realm dismantled was
     Of Jove himself; and now reigns here
         A very, very—pajock.   288

     Hor. You might have rimed.

     Ham. O good Horatio, I'll take the ghost's word for a thousand pound. Didst perceive?

     Hor. Very well, my lord.   292

     Ham. Upon the talk of the poisoning?

     Hor. I did very well note him.

     Ham. Ah, ha! Come, some music! come, the recorders!   296

     For if the king like not the comedy,
     Why then, belike he likes it not, perdy.

275 deer go weep; *cf. n.*
279 forest of feathers: *an allusion to the plumes worn by actors*
280 turn Turk: *play the renegade*
281 Provincial roses: *rosettes imitating the damask rose; cf. n.*
     razed: *slashed, i.e., with cuts or openings*
281–282 fellowship: *partnership*   cry: *company; cf. n.*
283 share: *i.e., in the profits of the company; cf. n.*
285 Damon; *cf. n.*   288 pajock: *scarecrow; cf. n.*
295 recorders: *wind instruments of the flute type*
298 perdy: *a corruption of* par dieu

Come, some music!

Enter Rosencrantz and Guildenstern.

Guil. Good my lord, vouchsafe me a word with
you.   300

Ham. Sir, a whole history.

Guil. The king, sir,—

Ham. Ay, sir, what of him?   303

Guil. Is in his retirement marvellous distempered.

Ham. With drink, sir?

Guil. No, my lord, with choler.   306

Ham. Your wisdom should show itself more richer
to signify this to the doctor; for, for me to put him
to his purgation would perhaps plunge him into
more choler.   310

Guil. Good my lord, put your discourse into some
frame, and start not so wildly from my affair.

Ham. I am tame, sir; pronounce.

Guil. The queen, your mother, in most great affliction of spirit, hath sent me to you.

Ham. You are welcome.   316

Guil. Nay, good my lord, this courtesy is not of
the right breed. If it shall please you to make me a
wholesome answer, I will do your mother's commandment; if not, your pardon and my return shall
be the end of my business.   321

Ham. Sir, I cannot.

Ros. What, my lord?

304 distempered: *disordered; cf. n.*
306 choler: *anger; cf. n.*   309 purgation: *purging; cf. n.*
312 frame: *sensible form*   313 pronounce: *speak*
318 of the right breed: *pure-bred, genuine; cf. n.*
319 wholesome: *sincere*

Ham. Make you a wholesome answer. My wit's diseased; but, sir, such answer as I can make, you shall command; or, rather, as you say, my mother. Therefore no more, but to the matter. My mother, you say,—   328

Ros. Then, thus she says: your behavior hath struck her into amazement and admiration.

Ham. O wonderful son, that can so 'stonish a mother! But is there no sequel at the heels of this mother's admiration? Impart.   333

Ros. She desires to speak with you in her closet ere you go to bed.

Ham. We shall obey, were she ten times our mother. Have you any further trade with us?

Ros. My lord, you once did love me.

Ham. And do still, by these pickers and stealers.

Ros. Good my lord, what is your cause of distemper? You do surely bar the door upon your own liberty, if you deny your griefs to your friend.   342

Ham. Sir, I lack advancement.

Ros. How can that be when you have the voice of the king himself for your succession in Denmark?

Enter the Players, with recorders.

Ham. Ay, sir, but 'While the grass grows,'—the proverb is something musty.—O, the recorders! Let me see one. To withdraw with you,—Why do you go

339 pickers and stealers: *hands; cf. n.*
342 liberty: *freedom of action*
344 voice: *vote* (cf. I. ii. 108 f.)
346 'While . . . grows'; *cf. n.*
348 withdraw with: *speak privately with*

about to recover the wind of me, as if you would
drive me into a toil?   350

Guil. O! my lord, if my duty be too bold, my love
is too unmannerly.

Ham. I do not well understand that. Will you
play upon this pipe?

Guil. My lord, I cannot.

Ham. I pray you.

Guil. Believe me, I cannot.   357

Ham. I do beseech you.

Guil. I know no touch of it, my lord.

Ham. It is as easy as lying. Govern these ventages
with your fingers and thumb, give it breath with
your mouth, and it will discourse most eloquent
music. Look you, these are the stops.

Guil. But these cannot I command to any utter-
ance of harmony. I have not the skill.   365

Ham. Why, look you now, how unworthy a thing
you make of me. You would play upon me; you
would seem to know my stops; you would pluck out
the heart of my mystery; you would sound me from
my lowest note to the top of my compass. And there
is much music, excellent voice, in this little organ,
yet cannot you make it speak. 'Sblood, do you think
I am easier to be played on than a pipe? Call me what
instrument you will, though you can fret me, yet you
cannot play upon me.   375

349 recover the wind of: *get advantage of; cf. n.*
350 toil: *snare*
359 know no touch: *have no skill at all; cf. n.*
360 ventages: *holes, stops*
370 compass: *range of voice*   374 fret; *cf. n.*

Enter Polonius.

God bless you, sir!

    Pol. My lord, the queen would speak with you, and presently.

    Ham. Do you see yonder cloud that's almost in shape of a camel?   380

    Pol. By the mass, and 'tis like a camel, indeed.

    Ham. Methinks it is like a weasel.

    Pol. It is backed like a weasel.   383

    Ham. Or like a whale?

    Pol. Very like a whale.

    Ham. Then I will come to my mother by and by. [*Aside.*] They fool me to the top of my bent. [*Aloud.*] I will come by and by.   388

    Pol. I will say so.   *Exit.*

    Ham. By and by is easily said. Leave me, friends.

            [*Exeunt all but Hamlet.*]

'Tis now the very witching time of night,   391
When churchyards yawn and hell itself breathes out
Contagion to this world. Now could I drink hot blood,
And do such bitter business as the day   394
Would quake to look on. Soft! now to my mother!
O heart, lose not thy nature; let not ever
The soul of Nero enter this firm bosom.
Let me be cruel, not unnatural;   398
I will speak daggers to her, but use none.
My tongue and soul in this be hypocrites:

386 by and by: *at once*
387 top . . . bent: *limit of my endurance; cf. n.*
391 witching: *when spells are cast*
397 Nero; *cf. n.*

How in my words somever she be shent,
To give them seals never, my soul, consent!　　402
　　　　　　　　　　　　　　　　　　Exit.

[SCENE THIRD.

A Room in the Castle]

Enter King, Rosencrantz, and Guildenstern.

King. I like him not, nor stands it safe with us
To let his madness range. Therefore prepare you.
I your commission will forthwith dispatch,
And he to England shall along with you.　　4
The terms of our estate may not endure
Hazard so near us as doth hourly grow
Out of his braves.

Guil.　　　　　We will ourselves provide.
Most holy and religious fear it is　　8
To keep those many many bodies safe
That live and feed upon your majesty.

Ros. The single and peculiar life is bound
With all the strength and armor of the mind　　12
To keep itself from noyance; but much more
That spirit upon whose weal depends and rests

401 How . . . somever; *cf.* I. v. 84　　shent: *rebuked*
402 give them seals: *confirm them by making words into deeds*
1 like him not: *distrust him*　　　2 range: *rove, roam*
3 forthwith dispatch: *prepare at once*　　5 terms: *condition*
7 braves: *defiances; cf. n.*　　　　　8 fear: *caution*
11 single and peculiar: *individual and private*
13 noyance: *harm*　　　　　　　14 weal: *welfare*

The lives of many. The cesse of majesty
Dies not alone, but like a gulf doth draw   16
What's near it with it. It is a massy wheel,
Fix'd on the summit of the highest mount,
To whose huge spokes ten thousand lesser things
Are mortis'd and adjoin'd; which, when it falls,   20
Each small annexment, petty consequence,
Attends the boisterous ruin. Never alone
Did the king sigh, but with a general groan.
 King. Arm you, I pray you, to this speedy voyage;   24
For we will fetters put about this fear,
Which now goes too free-footed.
 Ros.   We will haste us.
        Exeunt Gent[lemen].

     Enter Polonius.

 Pol. My lord, he's going to his mother's closet.
Behind the arras I'll convey myself   28
To hear the process. I'll warr'nt she'll tax him home;
And, as you said, and wisely was it said,
'Tis meet that some more audience than a mother,
Since nature makes them partial, should o'erhear   32
The speech, of vantage. Fare you well, my liege.
I'll call upon you ere you go to bed
And tell you what I know.
 King.   Thanks, dear my lord.
        Exit [Polonius].

---

15 cesse: *decease*   16 gulf: *whirlpool*
17–22 it is a massy wheel, *etc.; cf. n.*
21 annexment: *appendage*
22 Attends: *accompanies*   24 Arm: *prepare*
29 process: *interview* tax . . . home: *censure effectually*
30 as you said; *cf. n.*   33 of vantage: *in addition*

King tries to pray but he can not his sins are too heavy.

O my offence is rank, it smells to heaven!   36
It hath the primal eldest curse upon 't;
A brother's murther. Pray can I not.   *must repent to pray*
Though inclination be as sharp as will,
My stronger guilt defeats my strong intent,   40
And, like a man to double business bound,
I stand in pause where I shall first begin,
And both neglect. What if this cursed hand
Were thicker than itself with brother's blood,   44
Is there not rain enough in the sweet heavens
To wash it white as snow? Whereto serves mercy
But to confront the visage of offence?
And what's in prayer but this twofold force,   48
To be forestalled, ere we come to fall,
Or pardon'd, being down? Then I'll look up;
My fault is past. But, O, what form of prayer
Can serve my turn? 'Forgive me my foul murther?'   52
That cannot be, since I am still possess'd
Of those effects for which I did the murther,
My crown, mine own ambition, and my queen.
May one be pardon'd and retain th' offence?   56
In the corrupted currents of this world
Offence's gilded hand may shove by justice,
And oft 'tis seen the wicked prize itself

37 primal: *primeval; cf. n.*
44 thicker than itself: *made more than double its normal thickness*
47 confront: *oppose directly*
49 forestalled: *prevented in anticipation*
54 effects: i.e., *things acquired by an action*
55 ambition: i.e., *the realization of ambition* (so also offence in 56)
58 gilded hand: *hand using bribes of gold*
59 wicked prize: *reward of wickedness*

Buys out the law; but 'tis not so above.   60
There is no shuffling, there the action lies
In his true nature, and we ourselves compell'd
Even to the teeth and forehead of our faults
To give in evidence. What then? what rests?   64
Try what repentance can. What can it not?
Yet what can it, when one cannot repent?
O wretched state! O bosom black as death!
O limed soul, that struggling to be free   68
Art more engag'd! Help, angels! make assay!
Bow, stubborn knees; and heart with strings of steel
Be soft as sinews of the new-born babe.
All may be well.   *He kneels.*

Enter Hamlet.

[handwritten: Hamlet doesn't kill king Because he thinks he is praying + would go to heaven]

Ham. Now might I do it pat, now 'a is praying!   73
And now I'll do 't. And so 'a goes to heaven;
And so am I reveng'd? That would be scann'd.
A villain kills my father, and for that,   76
I, his sole son, do this same villain send
To heaven.
Why, this is hire and salary, not revenge.
'A took my father grossly, full of bread,   80
With all his crimes broad blown, as flush as May;

60 Buys out: *corrupts*
61 shuffling: *trickery*   lies: *used in its legal sense; cf. n.*
63 teeth and forehead: *very face*   64 rests: *remains*
68 limed: *caught with bird-lime*   69 engag'd: *entangled*
73 pat: *to a nicety; cf. n.*
75 would: *requires to*   scann'd: *examined, considered*
79 hire and salary: *i.e., a reward; cf. n.*
80 full of bread: *without opportunity to fast*
81 broad blown: *in full bloom*   flush: *lusty*

And how his audit stands who knows save heaven?
But in our circumstance and course of thought
'Tis heavy with him. And am I then reveng'd,   84
To take him in the purging of his soul,
When he is fit and season'd for his passage?
No.
Up, sword, and know thou a more horrid hent;   88
When he is drunk asleep, or in his rage,
Or in th' incestuous pleasure of his bed,
At game a-swearing, or about some act
That has no relish of salvation in 't.   92
Then trip him, that his heels may kick at heaven,
And that his soul may be as damn'd and black
As hell, whereto it goes. My mother stays.—
This physic but prolongs thy sickly days.   *Exit.*
   King [*rising*]. My words fly up, my thoughts remain
     below.   97
Words without thoughts never to heaven go.   *Exit.*

[SCENE FOURTH.

The Queen's Closet]

Enter Queen and Polonius.

   Pol. 'A will come straight. Look you lay home to him.
Tell him his pranks have been too broad to bear with,

82 audit: *account*
83 in . . . thought: *according to our vague ideas*
86 passage: i.e., *to the other world*
88 know . . . hent: *let me grasp you at a more horrid moment*
92 relish: *flavor*   96 physic: *medicine, i.e., the postponement*
1 lay home: *talk plainly*   2 broad: *free, unrestrained*

And that your Grace hath screen'd and stood between
Much heat and him. I'll silence me e'en here.   4
Pray you, be round with him.

    Ham. (*within.*) Mother, mother, mother!

    Queen.   I'll warrant you;
Fear me not. Withdraw, I hear him coming.

                  [*Polonius hides behind the arras.*]

Enter Hamlet

    Ham. Now, mother, what's the matter?   8
    Queen. Hamlet, thou hast thy father much offended.
    Ham. Mother, you have my father much offended.
    Queen. Come, come, you answer with an idle tongue.
    Ham. Go, go, you question with a wicked tongue.   12
    Queen. Why, how now, Hamlet!
    Ham.   What's the matter now?
    Queen. Have you forgot me?
    Ham.   No, by the rood, not so.
You are the queen, your husband's brother's wife;
And,—would it were not so!—you are my mother.   16
    Queen. Nay then, I'll set those to you that can speak.
    Ham. Come, come, and sit you down; you shall not
    budge.
You go not till I set you up a glass
Where you may see the inmost part of you.   20
    Queen. What wilt thou do? thou wilt not murther me?
Help, help, ho!
    Pol. What, ho! help! help! help!
    Ham. How now! a rat? Dead, for a ducat, dead!

                  Kills Polonius [*through the arras*].

---

4 heat: *anger*   silence me: *withdraw into silence*
14 rood: *cross*   24 for: *i.e., I wager*

Pol. O, I am slain!

Queen.   O me, what hast thou done?

Ham. Nay, I know not. Is it the king?

Queen. O, what a rash and bloody deed is this!

Ham. A bloody deed! almost as bad, good mother,   29
As kill a king, and marry with his brother.

Queen. As kill a king?

Ham.   Ay, lady, 'twas my word.

         [*Lifts up the arras and discovers Polonius.*]

Thou wretched, rash, intruding fool, farewell!
I took thee for thy better. Take thy fortune;   33
Thou find'st to be too busy is some danger.
[*To the Queen.*] Leave wringing of your hands. Peace!
     sit you down,
And let me wring your heart; for so I shall
If it be made of penetrable stuff,   37
If damned custom have not braz'd it so
That it be proof and bulwark against sense.

Queen. What have I done that thou dar'st wag thy
     tongue
In noise so rude against me?

Ham.   Such an act   41
That blurs the grace and blush of modesty,
Calls virtue hypocrite, takes off the rose
From the fair forehead of an innocent love
And sets a blister there, makes marriage vows
As false as dicers' oaths. O, such a deed   46
As from the body of contraction plucks

38 braz'd it: *made it brazen*
39 proof and bulwark: *an impenetrable defence*   sense: *feeling*
47 contraction: *marriage contract*

The very soul, and sweet religion makes
A rhapsody of words! Heaven's face does glow,
Yea, this solidity and compound mass,   50
With tristful visage as against the doom,
Is thought-sick at the act.
    Queen.   Ay me! what act,
That roars so loud and thunders in the index?
    Ham. Look here, upon this picture, and on this,   54
The counterfeit presentment of two brothers.
See what a grace was seated on this brow:
Hyperion's curls, the front of Jove himself,   57
An eye like Mars, to threaten and command,
A station like the herald Mercury
New-lighted on a heaven-kissing hill,
A combination and a form indeed,   61
Where every god did seem to set his seal,
To give the world assurance of a man.
This was your husband. Look you, now, what follows.
Here is your husband, like a mildew'd ear   65
Blasting his wholesome brother. Have you eyes?
Could you on this fair mountain leave to feed,
And batten on this moor? Ha! have you eyes?
You cannot call it love, for at your age   69
The heyday in the blood is tame, it's humble,

49 rhapsody: *meaningless string*   glow: *blush*
50 this solidity and compound mass: *the solid and composite earth*
51 tristful: *sad*   doom: *doomsday*
53 index: *table of contents, prelude*
55 counterfeit presentment: *portrayed likeness*
57 front: *forehead*   59 station: *poise*
65 ear: *ear of wheat*
68 batten: *grow fat*   moor: *a barren upland*
70 heyday: *youthful high spirits*

[margin, handwritten:] Hamlet contrasts pictures of the two brothers who were both kings

And waits upon the judgment; and what judgment
Would step from this to this? «Sense sure you have,
Else could you not have motion; but sure that sense
Is apoplex'd, for madness would not err,
Nor sense to ecstasy was ne'er so thrall'd
But it reserv'd some quantity of choice   76
To serve in such a difference.» What devil was 't
That thus hath cozen'd you at hoodman-blind?
«Eyes without feeling, feeling without sight,
Ears without hands or eyes, smelling sans all,
Or but a sickly part of one true sense   81
Could not so mope.»
O shame! where is thy blush? Rebellious hell,
If thou canst mutine in a matron's bones,
To flaming youth let virtue be as wax   85
And melt in her own fire: proclaim no shame
When the compulsive ardor gives the charge,
Since frost itself as actively doth burn,
And reason panders will.

    Queen.   O Hamlet, speak no more!
Thou turn'st mine eyes into my very soul;   90
And there I see such black and grained spots
As will not leave their tinct.

72 Sense: *control of the physical senses*
72–77 Sense . . . difference; *not in Folio*
74 apoplex'd: *atrophied*   75 thrall'd: *enslaved*
76 quantity of choice: *power to choose*
78 cozen'd: *cheated*   hoodman-blind: *blind man's buff*
79–82 *not in Folio*   80 sans: *without*
82 mope: *act aimlessly*   84 mutine: *rise in mutiny*
87 charge: *command*
89 panders: *ministers to the gratifications of*
91 grained: *ingrained*   92 leave their tinct: *lose their color*

Ham.   Nay, but to live   92
In the rank sweat of an enseamed bed,
Stew'd in corruption, honeying and making love
Over the nasty sty,
Queen.   O speak to me no more!
These words like daggers enter in my ears.   96
No more, sweet Hamlet!
Ham.   A murtherer and a villain;
A slave that is not twentieth part the tithe
Of your precedent lord; a vice of kings;
A cutpurse of the empire and the rule,
That from a shelf the precious diadem stole,   101
And put it in his pocket!
Queen.   No more!

Enter Ghost.   — to arouse interest

Ham. A king of shreds and patches,—
Save me, and hover o'er me with your wings,
You heavenly guards! What would your gracious figure?
Queen. Alas! he's mad!   106
Ham. Do you not come your tardy son to chide,
That, laps'd in time and passion, lets go by
Th' important acting of your dread command?
O, say.   — ghost or conscience?
Ghost.   Do not forget. This visitation   110
Is but to whet thy almost blunted purpose.
But, look, amazement on thy mother sits.

Hamlet sees ghost —
Queen does not

93 enseamed: *greasy*   94 honeying: *talking sweetly*
98 tithe: *tenth part (i.e., not one two-hundredth)*
99 precedent: *former*   vice: *buffoon; cf. n.*
100 cutpurse: *pickpocket*   103 shreds and patches; *cf. n.*
108 laps'd in time and passion: *frittering away time and energy*
109 important: *urgent*

O, step between her and her fighting soul.
Conceit in weakest bodies strongest works.
Speak to her, Hamlet.

   Ham.   How is it with you, lady?
   Queen. Alas, how is 't with you,
That you do bend your eye on vacancy   117
And with th' incorporal air do hold discourse?
Forth at your eyes your spirits wildly peep;
And, as the sleeping soldiers in th' alarm,
Your bedded hair, like life in excrements,   121
Start up and stand an end. O gentle son,
Upon the heat and flame of thy distemper
Sprinkle cool patience. Whereon do you look?
   Ham. On him, on him! Look you, how pale he glares!
His form and cause conjoin'd, preaching to stones, 126
Would make them capable.—Do not look upon me;
Lest with this piteous action you convert
My stern effects. Then what I have to do
Will want true color,—tears perchance for blood.   130
   Queen. To whom do you speak this?
   Ham.   Do you see nothing there?
   Queen. Nothing at all; yet all that is I see.
   Ham. Nor did you nothing hear?
   Queen.   No, nothing but ourselves.
   Ham. Why, look you there! look, how it steals away!

114 Conceit: *imagination*
118 incorporal: *incorporeal*
121 bedded: *smooth, flatly brushed*   hair: *hairs*   life in excrements: *dead tissue come alive*
122 an end: *on end*   126 conjoin'd: *united*
127 capable: *capable of feeling*   128 convert: *translate*
129 My stern effects: *the sternness of my deeds*
130 want true color: *not be what it should*

My father, in his habit as he liv'd!   135
Look, where he goes, even now, out at the portal.

Exit Ghost.

Queen. This is the very coinage of your brain: 137
This bodiless creation ecstasy
Is very cunning in.
    Ham.   ⟨Ecstasy!⟩
My pulse, as yours, doth temperately keep time,
And makes as healthful music. It is not madness   141
That I have utter'd. Bring me to the test,
And I the matter will re-word, which madness
Would gambol from. Mother, for love of grace,
Lay not that flattering unction to your soul,   145
That not your trespass but my madness speaks.
It will but skin and film the ulcerous place,
Whiles rank corruption, mining all within,   148
Infects unseen. Confess yourself to heaven;
Repent what's past; avoid what is to come;
And do not spread the compost on the weeds
To make them ranker. Forgive me this my virtue,   152
For in the fatness of these pursy times
Virtue itself of vice must pardon beg,
Yea, curb and woo for leave to do him good.
    Queen. O Hamlet, thou hast cleft my heart in twain.
    Ham. O throw away the worser part of it,   157
And live the purer with the other half.

135 habit . . . liv'd: *familiar costume*
139 Ecstasy; *not in Quarto*
143 re-word: *repeat word for word*
144 gambol from: *skip away from*   grace: *God*
145 unction: *salve*   148 mining: *undermining*
153 fatness: *grossness*   pursy: *corpulent*
155 curb and woo: *bow and beg*   him; *i.e., vice*

Good night; but go not to my uncle's bed;
Assume a virtue, if you have it not.   160
«That monster, custom, who all sense doth eat
Of habits evil, is angel yet in this,
That to the use of actions fair and good
He likewise gives a frock or livery   164
That aptly is put on.» Refrain to-night,
And that shall lend a kind of easiness
To the next abstinence: «the next more easy;
For use almost can change the stamp of nature,   168
And either [tame] the devil or throw him out
With wondrous potency.» Once more, good night,
And when you are desirous to be bless'd,
I'll blessing beg of you. For this same lord,   172
I do repent; but heaven hath pleas'd it so,
To punish me with this, and this with me,
That I must be their scourge and minister.
I will bestow him, and will answer well   176
The death I gave him. So, again, good night.
I must be cruel only to be kind:
Thus bad begins and worse remains behind.
«One word more, good lady.»
   Queen.   What shall I do?   180
   Ham. Not this, by no means, that I bid you do:
Let the bloat king tempt you again to bed,
Pinch wanton on your cheek, call you his mouse;

161–165 That . . . put on; *not in Folio*
162 evil: *'deuill' in Quarto*   163 use: *habitual practice*
167–170 the next . . . potency; *not in Folio*
169 tame; *cf. n.*   171 be bless'd: *become blessed*
176 answer: *account for*
180 One . . . lady; *not in Folio*
182 bloat: *bloated*   183 wanton: *wantonly*

And let him, for a pair of reechy kisses, 184
Or paddling in your neck with his damn'd fingers,
Make you to ravel all this matter out,
That I essentially am not in madness,
But mad in craft. 'Twere good you let him know; 188
For who that's but a queen, fair, sober, wise,
Would from a paddock, from a bat, a gib,
Such dear concernings hide? who would do so?
No, in despite of sense and secrecy, 192
Unpeg the basket on the house's top,
Let the birds fly, and, like the famous ape,
To try conclusions in the basket creep,
And break your own neck down. 196

Queen. Be thou assur'd, if words be made of breath,
And breath of life, I have no life to breathe
What thou hast said to me.

Ham. I must to England; you know that?

Queen. Alack!
I had forgot. 'Tis so concluded on. 201

Ham. «There's letters seal'd, and my two school-
fellows,
Whom I will trust as I will adders fang'd,
They bear the mandate; they must sweep my way
And marshal me to knavery. Let it work, 205
For 'tis the sport to have the enginer

184 reechy: *greasy* 185 paddling: *playing fondly*
187 essentially: *in my essential nature*
190 paddock: *toad* gib: *tom-cat*
191 dear concernings: *affairs dearly concerning one*
194 the famous ape; *cf. n.* 195 conclusions: *experiments*
196 down: *in the fall* 202–210 *not in Folio*
204 mandate: *command* sweep my way: *clear my path*
205 marshal: *conduct*
206 enginer: *maker of military engines, sapper*

Hoist with his own petar; and 't shall go hard
But I will delve one yard below their mines,   208
And blow them at the moon. O 'tis most sweet,
When in one line two crafts directly meet!»
This man shall set me packing.
I'll lug the guts into the neighbor room.—   212
Mother, good night indeed.—This counsellor
Is now most still, most secret, and most grave,
Who was in life a foolish prating knave.
Come, sir, to draw toward an end with you.   216
Good night, mother.

Exit Hamlet tugging in Polonius.

[SCENE FIFTH.

A Room in the Castle]

*Enter King and Queen, with Rosencrantz and
Guildenstern.*

   King. There's matter in these sighs, these profound
      heaves,
You must translate. 'Tis fit we understand them.
Where is your son?
   Queen. «Bestow this place on us a little while.»   4
            [*Exeunt Rosencrantz and Guildenstern.*]
Ah, mine own lord, what have I seen to-night!

207 Hoist: *blown up*   petar: *small bomb*
207–8 't shall . . . will: *it shall not be for lack of trying if I
   do not*   211 set me packing; *cf. n.*
III.v.s.d. *From this point to the end of Act Fourth, the act and
scene divisions differ from those traditionally employed; cf. note
to IV.i.s.d. The traditional numbering is indicated within square
brackets in the running heads.*
1 heaves: *prolonged sighs*   4 *Not in Folio; cf. n.*

King. What, Gertrude? How does Hamlet?

Queen. Mad as the sea and wind, when both contend
Which is the mightier. In his lawless fit,   8
Behind the arras hearing something stir,
Whips out his rapier, cries, 'A rat! a rat!'
And in this brainish apprehension kills
The unseen good old man.

King.   O heavy deed!   12
It had been so with us had we been there.
His liberty is full of threats to all;
To you yourself, to us, to every one.
Alas, how shall this bloody deed be answer'd?   16
It will be laid to us, whose providence
Should have kept short, restrain'd, and out of haunt,
This mad young man. But so much was our love,
We would not understand what was most fit,   20
But like the owner of a foul disease,
To keep it from divulging, let it feed
Even on the pith of life. Where is he gone?

Queen. To draw apart the body he hath kill'd,   24
O'er whom his very madness, like some ore
Among a mineral of metals base,
Shows itself pure. 'A weeps for what is done.

King. O Gertrude, come away!   28
The sun no sooner shall the mountains touch
But we will ship him hence; and this vile deed
We must with all our majesty and skill
Both countenance and excuse. Ho, Guildenstern!   32

7 Mad as the sea and wind; *cf. n.*
11 brainish apprehension: *insane illusion*
12 heavy: *grievous*   17 providence: *foresight*
18 short: *tethered*   out of haunt: *out of company*
22 divulging: *becoming known*   26 mineral: *mine*

[handwritten margin note: King says Hamlet would have killed him instead of Polonius]

Enter Rosencrantz and Guildenstern.

Friends both, go join you with some further aid.
Hamlet in madness hath Polonius slain,
And from his mother's closet hath he dragg'd him.
Go seek him out; speak fair, and bring the body
Into the chapel. I pray you haste in this.   37
                          Exeunt Gentlemen.

Come, Gertrude, we'll call up our wisest friends;
And let them know both what we mean to do
And what's untimely done. [So, haply, slander,]
«Whose whisper o'er the world's diameter,   41
As level as the cannon to his blank
Transports his poison'd shot, may miss our name,
And hit the woundless air.» O, come away!   44
My soul is full of discord and dismay.   *Exeunt.*

[SCENE SIXTH.

Another Room in the Castle]

Enter Hamlet.

Ham. Safely stowed.
Gentlemen within. Hamlet! Lord Hamlet!
Ham. What noise? who calls on Hamlet?
O, here they come.   4

Enter Rosencrantz and Guildenstern.

36 fair: *courteously*   40 So, haply, slander; *cf. n.*
41–44 Whose . . . air; *not in Folio*
41 diameter: *extent from side to side*
42 level: *straight*   blank: *white spot in the centre of a target*

Ros. What have you done, my lord, with the dead body?

Ham. Compounded it with dust, whereto 'tis kin.

Ros. Tell us where 'tis, that we may take it thence
And bear it to the chapel.   8

Ham. Do not believe it.

Ros. Believe what?

Ham. That I can keep your counsel and not mine own. Besides, to be demanded of a sponge, what replication should be made by the son of a king?

Ros. Take you me for a sponge, my lord?   14

Ham. Ay, sir, that soaks up the king's countenance, his rewards, his authorities. But such officers do the king best service in the end. He keeps them, like an ape an apple, in the corner of his jaw; first mouthed, to be last swallowed. When he needs what you have gleaned, it is but squeezing you, and, sponge, you shall be dry again.   21

Ros. I understand you not, my lord.

Ham. I am glad of it. A knavish speech sleeps in a foolish ear.

Ros. My lord, you must tell us where the body is, and go with us to the king.   26

Ham. The body is with the king, but the king is not with the body. The king is a thing—

Guil. A thing, my lord!

Ham. Of nothing. Bring me to him. ⟨Hide fox, and all after.⟩   *Exeunt.*

12 to be demanded of: *on being questioned by*
13 replication: *reply*   15 countenance: *favor*
16 authorities: *offices of authority*
17–18 like an ape an apple; *cf. n.*   27 The . . . body; *cf. n.*
30 Hide fox, and all after: *signal cry in a children's game; cf. n.*

[SCENE SEVENTH.

Another Room in the Castle]

Enter King and two or three.

King. I have sent to seek him and to find the body.
How dangerous is it that this man goes loose!
Yet must not we put the strong law on him:
He's lov'd of the distracted multitude,   4
Who like not in their judgment but their eyes;
And where 'tis so, th' offender's scourge is weigh'd,
But never the offence. To bear all smooth and even,
This sudden sending him away must seem   *people* 8
Deliberate pause. Diseases desperate grown *are not*
By desperate appliance are reliev'd   *going to*
Or not at all.   *better themselves*

(*all symbols of*
disease & corruption)

Enter Rosencrantz.

How now! what hath befall'n?
Ros. Where the dead body is bestow'd, my lord,   12
We cannot get from him.
King.   But where is he?
Ros. Without, my lord, guarded, to know your pleasure.
King. Bring him before us.
Ros. Ho, Guildenstern! bring in my lord.   16

Enter Hamlet and Guildenstern.

6 scourge: *punishment*
7 bear: *execute*   smooth and even: *pleasantly and equably*
9 Deliberate pause: *judicially considered*
10 appliance: *remedy*

King. Now, Hamlet, where's Polonius?

Ham. At supper.

King. At supper! Where?   19

Ham. Not where he eats, but where 'a is eaten.
A certain convocation of politic worms are e'en at
him. Your worm is your only emperor for diet: we
fat all creatures else to fat us, and we fat ourselves
for maggots. Your fat king and your lean beggar is
but variable service,—two dishes, but to one table.
That's the end.

«*King.* Alas, alas!   27

Ham. A man may fish with the worm that hath eat
of a king, and eat of the fish that hath fed of that
worm.»

King. What dost thou mean by this?   31

Ham. Nothing, but to show you how a king may
go a progress through the guts of a beggar.

King. Where is Polonius?   34

Ham. In heaven. Send thither to see. If your messenger find him not there, seek him i' th' other place
yourself. But, indeed, if you find him not within this
month, you shall nose him as you go up the stairs
into the lobby.   39

King. [*To some Attendants.*] Go seek him there.

Ham. 'A will stay till you come.

                                      [*Exeunt Attendants.*]

King. Hamlet, this deed, for thine especial safety,—
Which we do tender, as we dearly grieve   43
For that which thou hast done,—must send thee hence

21 convocation: *assembly; cf. n.*   politic: *crafty*
25 variable service: *variety of courses*
27–30 *not in Folio*   33 progress: *state journey*

⟨With fiery quickness⟩.   Therefore prepare thyself.
The bark is ready and the wind at help,
Th' associates tend, and everything is bent   47
For England.

Ham.   For England?

King.   Ay, Hamlet.

Ham.   Good.

King. So is it, if thou knew'st our purposes.

  Ham. I see a cherub that sees them. But, come;
for England! Farewell, dear mother.   51

  King. Thy loving father, Hamlet.

  Ham. My mother. Father and mother is man and
wife, man and wife is one flesh, and so, my mother.
Come, for England!   *Exit.*

  King. Follow him at foot; tempt him with speed aboard.
Delay it not, I'll have him hence to-night.   57
Away! for everything is seal'd and done
That else leans on th' affair. Pray you, make haste.   59
            [*Exeunt Rosencrantz and Guildenstern.*]
And, England, if my love thou hold'st at aught,—
As my great power thereof may give thee sense,
Since yet thy cicatrice looks raw and red
After the Danish sword, and thy free awe   63
Pays homage to us,—thou mayst not coldly set
Our sovereign process, which imports at full,
By letters cóngruing to that effect,

---

45 With fiery quickness; *not in Quarto*   47 bent: *prepared*
56 at foot: *close behind*   59 leans on: *depends upon*
61 thereof may give thee sense: *may make you think of it*
62 cicatrice: *scar*
63 free awe: *awe still felt but no longer enforced by arms*
64 set: *esteem*
65 process: *formal command*   66 congruing: *agreeing*

The present death of Hamlet. Do it, England;
For like the hectic in my blood he rages,   68
And thou must cure me. Till I know 'tis done,
Howe'er my haps, my joys were ne'er begun.   *Exit.*

Orders England to murder Hamlet

[SCENE EIGHTH.

Open Country near the Castle]

Guess sense of order

Enter Fortinbras with his army over the stage.

For. Go, captain, from me greet the Danish king.
Tell him that by his licence Fortinbras
Craves the conveyance of a promis'd march
Over his kingdom. You know the rendezvous.   4
If that his majesty would aught with us,
We shall express our duty in his eye,
And let him know so.
 Cap.   I will do 't, my lord.
 For. Go softly on.

       Exit [with army, leaving Captain].

«*Enter Hamlet, Rosencrantz, &c.*

Ham. Good sir, whose powers are these?
Cap. They are of Norway, sir.
Ham. How purpos'd, sir, I pray you?
Cap. Against some part of Poland.   12
Ham. Who commands them, sir?
Cap. The nephew to old Norway, Fortinbras.

68 hectic: *wasting fever*   70 haps: *fortunes*
3 the conveyance of: *escort during the course of*
6 in his eye: *in his presence* 8 softly: *slowly*
9–66 *not in Folio*   9 powers: *troops*

Ham. Goes it against the main of Poland, sir,
Or for some frontier?   16
Cap. Truly to speak, and with no addition,
We go to gain a little patch of ground
That hath in it no profit but the name.
To pay five ducats, five, I would not farm it;   20
Nor will it yield to Norway or the Pole
A ranker rate, should it be sold in fee.
Ham. Why, then the Polack never will defend it.
Cap. Yes, it is already garrison'd.   24
Ham. Two thousand souls and twenty thousand ducats
Will not debate the question of this straw.
This is th' imposthume of much wealth and peace,
That inward breaks, and shows no cause without   28
Why the man dies. I humbly thank you, sir.
Cap. God be wi' you, sir.   [*Exit.*]
Ros.   Will 't please you go, my lord?
Ham. I'll be with you straight. Go a little before.

[*Exeunt all except Hamlet.*]

How all occasions do inform against me   32
And spur my dull revenge! What is a man,
If his chief good and market of his time
Be but to sleep and feed? A beast, no more.
Sure he that made us with such large discourse,   36
Looking before and after, gave us not
That capability and godlike reason
To fust in us unus'd. Now, whether it be

15 main: *chief part*
17 no addition: *without adding fine words*
22 ranker: *richer*   sold in fee: *sold absolutely*
26 debate: *bring to a settlement*   straw: *trifling matter*
27 imposthume: *abscess*   34 market of: *way to dispose of*
36 large discourse: *latitude of comprehension*
39 fust: *become mouldy*

Bestial oblivion, or some craven scruple   40
Of thinking too precisely on th' event
(A thought, which, quarter'd, hath but one part wisdom,
And ever three parts coward) I do not know
Why yet I live to say 'This thing's to do,'   44
Sith I have cause and will and strength and means
To do 't. Examples gross as earth exhort me:
Witness this army of such mass and charge,
Led by a delicate and tender prince,   48
Whose spirit with divine ambition puff'd
Makes mouths at the invisible event,
Exposing what is mortal and unsure
To all that fortune, death and danger dare,   52
Even for an egg-shell. Rightly to be great
Is not to stir without great argument,
But greatly to find quarrel in a straw
When honor's at the stake. How stand I then,
That have a father kill'd, a mother stain'd,   57
Excitements of my reason and my blood,
And let all sleep, while, to my shame, I see
The imminent death of twenty thousand men,
That for a fantasy and trick of fame   61
Go to their graves like beds, fight for a plot
Whereon the numbers cannot try the cause,
Which is not tomb enough and continent   64
To hide the slain? O, from this time forth,
My thoughts be bloody, or be nothing worth!   *Exit.*»

40 Bestial oblivion: *animal-like forgetfulness*
41 event: *outcome*   44 to do; *i.e., still undone*
46 gross: *weighty*   47 charge: *expense*
54 argument: *cause*   58 Excitements: *incentives*
61 trick: *trifle*   64 continent: (*a sufficient*) *receptacle*

[ACT FOURTH

SCENE FIRST.

A Room in the Castle]

Ophelia has gone mad after hearing of fathers death

Enter Queen, Horatio, and a Gentleman.

Queen. I will not speak with her.

Gent. She is importunate, indeed distract:
Her mood will needs be pitied.

Queen.   What would she have?

Gent. She speaks much of her father; says she hears   4
There's tricks i' th' world; and hems, and beats her heart;
Spurns enviously at straws, speaks things in doubt
That carry but half sense. Her speech is nothing,
Yet the unshaped use of it doth move   8
The hearers to collection. They aim at it,
And botch the words up fit to their own thoughts;
Which, as her winks and nods and gestures yield them,
Indeed would make one think there might be thought,
Though nothing sure, yet much unhappily.   13

Hor. 'Twere good she were spoken with, for she may
    strew

Scene First, S. d.; *cf. n.*
2 importunate: *persistent*   5 tricks: *deceptions*
6 Spurns: *kicks*   enviously: *spitefully*   in doubt: *ambiguous*
8 unshaped: *artless*
9 collection: *inference*   aim: *guess*
11 Which: *the words*   yield them: *interpret her words*
13 nothing: *not at all*   much: *very*

Dangerous conjectures in ill-breeding minds.

    Queen. Let her come in.   [*Exit Gentleman.*]

To my sick soul, as sin's true nature is,   17

Each toy seems prologue to some great amiss.

So full of artless jealousy is guilt,

It spills itself in fearing to be spilt.   20

Enter Ophelia distracted.

  Oph. Where is the beauteous majesty of Denmark?

  Queen. How now, Ophelia!   *She sings.*

    Oph. How should I your true love know
        From another one?   24
      By his cockle hat and staff,
        And his sandal shoon.

  Queen. Alas! sweet lady, what imports this song?

  Oph. Say you? nay, pray you, mark.   *Song.* 28

      He is dead and gone, lady,
        He is dead and gone;
      At his head a grass-green turf;
        At his heels a stone.   32

O, ho!

  Queen. Nay, but Ophelia,—

  Oph. Pray you, mark.

      White his shroud as the mountain snow,—   36

Enter King.

  Queen. Alas! look here, my lord.

---

15 ill-breeding: *plotting ill*   18 great amiss: *calamity*
19 artless jealousy: *foolish anxiety*
20 spills: *ruins*   S. d. *Cf. n.*
25 cockle hat: *pilgrim's hat; cf. n.*   26 shoon: *shoes*

Oph.   Larded all with sweet flowers;   *Song.*
     Which bewept to the ground did—not—go
       With true-love showers.   40

King. How do you, pretty lady?

Oph. Well, God 'ild you! They say the owl was a baker's daughter. Lord! we know what we are, but know not what we may be. God be at your table!   45

     King. Conceit upon her father.

Oph. Pray, let's have no words of this; but when they ask you what it means, say you this:

     To-morrow is Saint Valentine's day,   49
       All in the morning betime,
     And I a maid at your window,
       To be your Valentine.   52
     Then up he rose, and donn'd his clo'es,
       And dupp'd the chamber door;
     Let in the maid, that out a maid
       Never departed more.   56

King. Pretty Ophelia!

Oph. Indeed, la, without an oath, I'll make an end on 't:

     By Gis and by Saint Charity,
       Alack, and fie for shame!   60
     Young men will do 't, if they come to 't;
       By Cock they are to blame.
     Quoth she, before you tumbled me,
       You promis'd me to wed.   64

---

38 Larded: *garnished*   39 did—not—go; *cf. n.*
42 God 'ild: *God reward*   owl was a baker's daughter; *cf. n.*
54 dupp'd: *opened*
59 by Gis: *by Jesus*   62 Cock: *perversion of 'God' in oaths*

He answers:

So would I ha' done, by yonder sun,
    An thou hadst not come to my bed.

King. How long hath she been thus?   67
    Oph. I hope all will be well. We must be pa-
tient; but I cannot choose but weep to think they
would lay him i' th' cold ground. My brother
shall know of it: and so I thank you for your
good counsel. Come, my coach! Good night, la-
dies; good night, sweet ladies; good night, good
night.   *Exit.*
King. Follow her close. Give her good watch, I pray
    you.   [*Exit Horatio.*]
O, this is the poison of deep grief; it springs   76
All from her father's death. O Gertrude, Gertrude!
When sorrows come, they come not single spies,
But in battalions. First, her father slain;
Next, your son gone, and he most violent author   80
Of his own just remove; the people muddied,
Thick and unwholesome in their thoughts and whispers
For good Polonius' death,—and we have done but greenly,
In hugger-mugger to inter him; poor Ophelia
Divided from herself and her fair judgment,   85
Without the which we are pictures, or mere beasts.
Last, and as much containing as all these,
Her brother is in secret come from France,   88
Feeds on his wonder, keeps himself in clouds,
And wants not buzzers to infect his ear

81 remove: *removal*   muddied: *stirred up*
83 greenly: *foolishly*   84 In hugger-mugger: *secretly*
89 wonder: *doubt*   in clouds: *in gloom,* or, *invisible*
90 buzzers: *tale-bearers*

With pestilent speeches of his father's death;
Wherein necessity, of matter beggar'd,   92
Will nothing stick our person to arraign
In ear and ear. O my dear Gertrude, this,
Like to a murdering-piece, in many places
Gives me superfluous death.   *A noise within.*

   ⟨Queen.   Alack! what noise is this?⟩
   King. «Attend!»

Laertes comes and is calmed by Claudius

                    Enter a Messenger.

Where are my Switzers? Let them guard the door.   97
What is the matter?
   Mess.   Save yourself, my lord!
The ocean, overpeering of his list,
Eats not the flats with more impetuous haste
Than young Laertes, in a riotous head,   101
O'erbears your officers. The rabble call him lord,
And as the world were now but to begin,
Antiquity forgot, custom not known,   104
The ratifiers and props of every word,
They cry, 'Choose we! Laertes shall be king!'
Caps, hands, and tongues applaud it to the clouds,
'Laertes shall be king, Laertes king!'   108
                    A noise within.
   Queen. How cheerfully on the false trail they cry!

92 Wherein: *i.e., in which pestilent speeches*   necessity:
     poverty (of argument)
93 nothing stick: *not at all hesitate*
94 In ear and ear: *in many ears*
95 murdering-piece: *small 'anti-personnel' cannon*
97 Switzers: *Swiss guards; cf. n.*
99 overpeering: *rising above*   list: *boundary*
101 head: *hostile advance*

O, this is counter, you false Danish dogs!
    King. The doors are broke.

             Enter Laertes with others.

    Laer. Where is this king? Sirs, stand you all without.
    All. No, let's come in.   113
    Laer.   I pray you, give me leave.
    All. We will! we will!
    Laer.   I thank you: keep the door. [*Mob retires.*]
O thou vile king!
Give me my father.
    Queen.   Calmly, good Laertes.   117
    Laer. That drop of blood that's calm proclaims me
        bastard,
Cries cuckold to my father, brands the harlot
Even here, between the chaste unsmirched brows
Of my true mother.
    King. Plays innocent (naïve) What is the cause, Laertes,
That thy rebellion looks so giantlike?   122
Let him go, Gertrude; do not fear our person.
There's such divinity doth hedge a king
That treason can but peep to what it would,
Acts little of his will. Tell me, Laertes,   126
Why thou art thus incens'd. Let him go, Gertrude.
Speak, man.
    Laer. Where is my father?
    King.   Dead.
    Queen.   But not by him.

110 counter: *following the trail in a direction opposite to that*
    which the game has taken
119 cuckold: *husband with an unfaithful wife*
125 peep: *look from tiptoe (as over a hedge)*

King. Let him demand his fill.   129
   Laer. How came he dead? I'll not be juggled with.
To hell, allegiance! vows, to the blackest devil!
Conscience and grace, to the profoundest pit!
I dare damnation. To this point I stand,   133
That both the worlds I give to negligence.
Let come what comes! only I'll be reveng'd
Most throughly for my father.
   King.   Who shall stay you?
   Laer. My will, not all the world: 137
And for my means, I'll husband them so well,
They shall go far with little.
   King.   Good Laertes,
If you desire to know the certainty
Of your dear father, is 't writ in your revenge,   141
That, swoopstake, you will draw both friend and foe,
Winner and loser?
   Laer. None but his enemies.
   King.   Will you know them then?
   Laer. To his good friends thus wide I'll ope my
      arms;   145
And like the kind life-rendering pelican,
Repast them with my blood.
   King.   Why, now you speak
Like a good child and a true gentleman.
That I am guiltless of your father's death,   149

132 grace: *God's grace*
134 both the worlds: *this world and the next*
137 My will: *as regards my will*
140 certainty: *the real truth*
142 swoopstake: *indiscriminately; cf. n.*
146 life-rendering pelican; *cf. n.*
147 Repast: *feed*

And am most sensibly in grief for it,
It shall as level to your judgment peer
As day does to your eye.
   A noise within. [*Voices.*] Let her come in.
   Laer. How now! what noise is that?   153

             Enter Ophelia.

O heat, dry up my brains! tears seven times salt,
Burn out the sense and virtue of mine eye!
By heaven, thy madness shall be paid with weight,
Till our scale turn the beam. O rose of May!
Dear maid, kind sister, sweet Ophelia!   158
O heavens! is 't possible a young maid's wits
Should be as mortal as an old man's life?
⟨Nature is fine in love, and where 'tis fine   161
It sends some precious instance of itself
After the thing it loves.⟩

   Oph. They bore him barefac'd on the bier;   *Song.*
       Hey non nonny, nonny, hey nonny;   165
       And in his grave rain'd many a tear—

Fare you well, my dove!
   Laer. Hadst thou thy wits, and didst persuade revenge,
It could not move thus.   169

   Oph. You must sing, a-down a-down,
       And you call him a-down-a.

O how the wheel becomes it! It is the false steward
that stole his master's daughter.   173

150 sensibly: *feelingly*   151 peer: *show itself*
155 sense and virtue: *feeling and power*
156 paid with weight: *heavily paid for*
157 of May: *early-blooming, delicate*
161–163 *not in Quarto; cf. n.*   165 Hey non nonny; *cf. n.*
172 wheel; *cf. n.*   false steward; *cf. n.*

Laer. This nothing's more than matter.

Oph. There's rosemary, that's for remembrance;
pray you, love, remember: and there is pansies, that's
for thoughts.   177

Laer. A document in madness, thoughts and remembrance fitted.

Oph. There's fennel for you, and columbines;
there's rue for you, and here's some for me; we may
call it herb of grace o' Sundays. O, you must wear
your rue with a difference. There's a daisy; I would
give you some violets, but they withered all when
my father died. They say he made a good end.   185

For bonny sweet Robin is all my joy.

Laer. Thought and affliction, passion, hell itself,
She turns to favor and to prettiness.   188

Oph.   And will 'a not come again?   *Song.*
              And will 'a not come again?
                No, no, he is dead;
                Go to thy deathbed,   192
              He never will come again.
              His beard was as white as snow
              All flaxen was his poll,
                He is gone, he is gone,   196
                And we castaway moan:
              God ha' mercy on his soul!

175 rosemary; *cf. n.*
176 pansies; *cf. n.*   178 document: *lesson*
180 fennel: *emblem of flattery*   columbines: *emblems of*
    thanklessness   181 rue: *emblem of repentance; cf. n.*
183 difference; *cf. n.*   daisy: *emblem of dissemblers*
184 violets: *emblems of faithfulness*
186 For . . . joy; *cf. n.*   187 passion: *suffering*
188 favor: *charm*   195 poll: *head ('pow' in dialect)*
197 castaway: *bereaved ones*

And of all Christian souls, I pray God. God be wi'
you!   *Exit Ophelia*

Laer. Do you see this, O God?   201

King. Laertes, I must cómmune with your grief,
Or you deny me right. Go but apart,
Make choice of whom your wisest friends you will,   204
And they shall hear and judge 'twixt you and me.
If by direct or by collateral hand
They find us touch'd, we will our kingdom give,
Our crown, our life, and all that we call ours   208
To you in satisfaction; but if not,
Be you content to lend your patience to us,
And we shall jointly labor with your soul
To give it due content.

Laer.   Let this be so.   212
His means of death, his óbscure burial,
No trophy, sword, nor hatchment o'er his bones,
No noble rite nor formal ostentation,
Cry,—to be heard as 'twere from heaven to earth,—
That I must call 't in question.

King.   So you shall;   217
And where th' offence is let the great axe fall.
I pray you go with me.   *Exeunt.*

202 commune: *consult*
203 right: *equitable treatment*
204 whom your: *whichever*
206 collateral: *indirect*
207 touch'd: *implicated*
213 means: *manner*
214 trophy: *memorial emblem*   hatchment: *tablet displaying
      armorial bearings*
215 ostentation: *ceremony*
216 Cry: *cry out, proclaim*   to be heard: *so loud as to be heard*
217 call 't in question: *demand an explanation*

[SCENE SECOND.

Another Room in the Castle]

Enter Horatio with an Attendant.

Hor. What are they that would speak with me?

Atten. Seafaring men, sir. They say they have letters
   for you.

Hor. Let them come in. [*Exit Attendant.*]
I do not know from what part of the world 4
I should be greeted, if not from Lord Hamlet.

Enter Sailor.

Sail. God bless you, sir.
Hor. Let him bless thee too.
Sail. 'A shall, sir, an 't please him. There's a letter
for you, sir. It came from th' ambassador that was
bound for England,—if your name be Horatio, as I
am let to know it is. 11

Hor. (*reads the letter*). Horatio, when thou shalt have
overlooked this, give these fellows some means to the
king: they have letters for him. Ere we were two days old
at sea, a pirate of very warlike appointment gave us chase.
Finding ourselves too slow of sail, we put on a compelled
valor, and in the grapple I boarded them. On the instant
they got clear of our ship, so I alone became their prisoner. They have dealt with me like thieves of mercy, but
they knew what they did; I am to do a good turn for them.
Let the king have the letters I have sent, and repair thou

13 overlooked: *perused*
15 appointment: *equipment*   21 repair: *come*

to me with as much speed as thou wouldst fly death. I
have words to speak in thine ear will make thee dumb;
yet are they much too light for the bore of the matter.
These good fellows will bring thee where I am. Rosencrantz
and Guildenstern hold their course for England. Of them I
have much to tell thee. Farewell.

> He that thou knowest thine,
>   Hamlet.

Come, I will give you way for these your letters,   29
And do 't the speedier that you may direct me
To him from whom you brought them.   *Exeunt.*

[SCENE THIRD.

A Room in the Castle]

Enter King and Laertes.

King. Now must your conscience my acquittance seal,
And you must put me in your heart for friend,
Sith you have heard, and with a knowing ear,
That he which hath your noble father slain   4
Pursu'd my life.

Laer.   It well appears; but tell me
Why you proceeded not against these feats,
So crimeful and so capital in nature,
As by your safety, greatness, wisdom, all things,   8

24 bore: *literally, calibre, hence importance*
29 way: *passage*
3 knowing: *convinced*   5 Pursu'd: *sought*
7 capital: *punishable by death*
8 your safety: *regard for your safety*   greatness: *position*
    wisdom: *intelligence in general; cf. n.*

You mainly were stirr'd up.

   King.   O, for two special reasons,
Which may to you perhaps seem much unsinew'd,
But yet to me they 're strong. The queen his mother
Lives almost by his looks, and for myself,—   12
My virtue or my plague, be it either which,—
She's so conjunctive to my life and soul
That, as the star moves not but in his sphere,
I could not but by her. The other motive   16
Why to a public count I might not go
Is the great love the general gender bear him,
Who, dipping all his faults in their affection,
Work like the spring that turneth wood to stone,—   20
Convert his gyves to graces; so that my arrows,
Too slightly timber'd for so loud a wind,
Would have reverted to my bow again,
And not where I had aim'd them.   24

   Laer. And so have I a noble father lost,
A sister driven into desperate terms,
Whose worth, if praises may go back again,
Stood challenger-on-mount of all the age   28
For her perfections. But my revenge will come.

9 mainly: *strongly*   10 unsinew'd: *weak*
13 be . . . which: *whichever it be*
14 conjunctive: *closely united*
16 could not but by her: *could not move except beside her,*
    (*could not live without her*)
17 count: *legal indictment*
18 general gender: *common people*
20 Work; *cf. n.*   spring; *cf. n.*
21 gyves: *leg-irons, marks of shame*
22 Too slightly timber'd: *too light*
23 reverted: *returned; cf. n.*   27 praises . . . again; *cf. n.*
28 challenger-on-mount: *mounted challenger, ready in the lists;*
    cf. n.

King. Break not your sleeps for that. You must not think
That we are made of stuff so flat and dull
That we can let our beard be shook with danger
And think it pastime. You shortly shall hear more.   33
I lov'd your father, and we love ourself,
And that, I hope, will teach you to imagine,—

Enter a Messenger with letters.

⟨How now, what news?
    Mess.   Letters, my lord, from Hamlet.⟩
These to your majesty; this to the queen.   37
    King. From Hamlet? who brought them?
    Mess. Sailors, my lord, they say; I saw them not.
They were given me by Claudio, he receiv'd them   40
«Of him that brought them.»
    King.   Laertes, you shall hear them.—
Leave us.   *Exit Messenger.*

High and mighty, you shall know I am set naked on
your kingdom. To-morrow shall I beg leave to see your
kingly eyes; when I shall (first asking your pardon there-
unto) recount the occasion of my sudden and more strange
return.

What should this mean? Are all the rest come back?   48
Or is it some abuse, and no such thing?
    Laer. Know you the hand?
    King.   'Tis Hamlet's character. 'Naked'!
And in a postscript here, he says, 'alone.'   51
Can you advise me?

36 *not in Quarto*   40 Claudio; *cf. n.*
41 Of . . . them; *not in Folio*   43 naked: *without resources*
49 abuse: *imposture*   50 character: *handwriting*

Laer. I'm lost in it, my lord. But let him come!
It warms the very sickness in my heart
That I shall live and tell him to his teeth,   55
'Thus didest thou.'

    King.   If it be so, Laertes,—
As how should it be so? how otherwise?—
Will you be rul'd by me?

    Laer.   Ay, my lord;
So you will not o'er-rule me to a peace.   59

    King. To thine own peace. If he be now return'd,
As checking at his voyage, and that he means
No more to undertake it, I will work him
To an exploit now ripe in my device,   63
Under the which he shall not choose but fall;
And for his death no wind of blame shall breathe,
But even his mother shall uncharge the practice
And call it accident.

    «*Laer.*   My lord, I will be rul'd;   67
The rather, if you could devise it so
That I might be the organ.

    King.   It falls right.
You have been talk'd of since your travel much,
And that in Hamlet's hearing, for a quality   71
Wherein, they say, you shine. Your sum of parts
Did not together pluck such envy from him
As did that one, and that, in my regard,
Of the unworthiest siege.

    Laer.   What part is that, my lord?   75

61 checking: *stopping short*
66 uncharge: *acquit of guilt*   practice: *stratagem*
67–80 Laer. . . . graveness; *not in Folio*
69 organ: *instrument*   falls: *happens*
75 siege: *rank; cf. n.*   part: *attribute*

King. A very riband in the cap of youth,
Yet needful too, for youth no less becomes
The light and careless livery that it wears
Than settled age his sables and his weeds   79
Importing health and graveness.» Two months since
Here was a gentleman of Normandy.
I've seen myself, and serv'd against, the French,
And they can well on horseback; but this gallant   83
Had witchcraft in 't. He grew unto his seat,
And to such wondrous doing brought his horse,
As had he been incorps'd and demi-natur'd
With the brave beast. So far he topp'd my thought, 87
That I, in forgery of shapes and tricks,
Come short of what he did.
    Laer.   A Norman was 't?
    King. A Norman.
    Laer. Upon my life, Lamound.
    King.   The very same.   91
    Laer. I know him well. He is the brooch indeed
And gem of all the nation.
    King. He made confession of you,
And gave you such a masterly report   95
For art and exercise in your defence,
And for your rapier most especially,
That he cried out, 'twould be a sight indeed

---

76 riband: *ribbon*   78 livery: *garb*
79 weeds: *garments*   80 health: *prosperity*
83 can well: *are skilled*
86 incorps'd and demi-natur'd; *cf. n.*   87 topp'd: *surpassed*
88 in . . . tricks: *cf. n.*   91 Lamound; *cf. n.*
94 confession: *report*   95 masterly report; *cf. n.*
96 art and exercise: *theory and practice*   defence: *science of*
    defence

IV : 3[IV : 7]

If one could match you. «The scrimers of their nation,
He swore, had neither motion, guard, nor eye,   100
If you oppos'd them.» Sir, this report of his
Did Hamlet so envenom with his envy
That he could nothing do but wish and beg   103
Your sudden coming o'er, to play with you.
Now, out of this,—
    Laer.   What out of this, my lord?
    King. Laertes, was your father dear to you?
Or are you like the painting of a sorrow,   107
A face without a heart?
    Laer.   Why ask you this?
    King. Not that I think you did not love your father,
But that I know love is begun by time,
And that I see, in passages of proof,   111
Time qualifies the spark and fire of it.
«There lives within the very flame of love
A kind of wick or snuff that will abate it,
And nothing is at a like goodness still,   115
For goodness, growing to a plurisy,
Dies in his own too-much. That we would do,
We should do when we would, for this 'would' changes,
And hath abatements and delays as many   119
As there are tongues, are hands, are accidents;
And then this 'should' is like a spendthrift's sigh,
That hurts by easing. But, to the quick o' th' ulcer:»
Hamlet comes back. What would you undertake

99–101 The scrimers . . . them; *not in Folio*
99 scrimers: *fencers*   104 play: *fence; cf. n.*
111 passages of proof; *cf. n.*   113–122 *not in Folio*
116 plurisy: *fulness; cf. n.*
119 abatements: *diminutions*   121 spendthrift's sigh; *cf. n.*

To show yourself in deed your father's son   124
More than in words?

    Laer.   To cut his throat i' th' church.

    King. No place, indeed, should murther sanctuarize;
Revenge should have no bounds. But, good Laertes,   127
Will you do this: keep close within your chamber?
Hamlet return'd shall know you are come home.
We'll put on those shall praise your excellence,
And set a double varnish on the fame   131
The Frenchman gave you,—bring you, in fine, together,
And wager on your heads. He, being remiss,
Most generous, and free from all contriving,
Will not peruse the foils; so that with ease,   135
Or with a little shuffling, you may choose
A sword unbated, and in a pass of practice
Requite him for your father.

    Laer.   I will do 't;
And for that purpose I'll anoint my sword.   139
I bought an unction of a mountebank
So mortal that, but dip a knife in it,
Where it draws blood no cataplasm so rare,
Collected from all simples that have virtue   143
Under the moon, can save the thing from death
That is but scratch'd withal. I'll touch my point
With this contagion, that if I gall him slightly,
It may be death.

    King.   Let's further think of this,   147

130 put on: *instigate*   those: *certain persons who*
133 remiss: *easy-going*   135 peruse: *inspect*
137 unbated: *not blunted*   pass of practice: *treacherous thrust*
139 anoint: *smear*   140 mountebank; *cf. n.*
142 cataplasm: *poultice*
143 simples: *medicinal herbs*   144 moon; *cf. n.*

Weigh what convenience both of time and means
May fit us to our shape. If this should fail,
And that our drift look through our bad performance,
'Twere better not assay'd. Therefore this project   151
Should have a back or second, that might hold,
If this should blast in proof. Soft! let me see.
We'll make a solemn wager on your cunnings.
I ha 't: 155
When in your motion you are hot and dry,—
As make your bouts more violent to that end,—
And that he calls for drink, I'll have prepar'd him
A chalice for the nonce, whereon but sipping,
If he by chance escape your venom'd stuck,   160
Our purpose may hold there. «But stay! what noise?»

Enter Queen.

(How, sweet queen?)

   Queen. One woe doth tread upon another's heel,   163
So fast they follow. Your sister's drown'd, Laertes.
   Laer. Drown'd! O, where?
   Queen. There is a willow grows aslant a brook,
That shows his hoar leaves in the glassy stream.
There with fantastic garlands did she come   168
Of crowflowers, nettles, daisies, and long purples,

149 our shape: *part we purpose to act*
150 drift . . . performance; *cf. n.*
152 a back or second; *cf. n.*
153 blast in proof: *burst when tested (as of a cannon)*
154 cunnings: *skill*   156 motion: *bodily exertion*
159 for the nonce: *for the purpose*
160 stuck: *thrust*   161 But . . . noise: *not in Folio*
162 *Not in Quarto*   167 hoar: *greyish-white*
169 crowflowers: *buttercups; cf. n.*   long purples: *early purple*
    orchids *(orchis mascula)*

That liberal shepherds give a grosser name,
But our cold maids do dead men's fingers call them.   171
There, on the pendent boughs her coronet weeds
Clambering to hang, an envious sliver broke,
When down her weedy trophies and herself
Fell in the weeping brook. Her clothes spread wide,   175
And mermaid-like awhile they bore her up;
Which time she chanted snatches of old tunes,
As one incapable of her own distress,
Or like a creature native and indu'd   179
Unto that element; but long it could not be
Till that her garments, heavy with their drink,
Pull'd the poor wretch from her melodious lay
To muddy death.

    Laer.   Alas, then, she is drown'd?   183
    Queen. Drown'd, drown'd.
    Laer. Too much of water hast thou, poor Ophelia,
And therefore I forbid my tears; but yet
It is our trick, nature her custom holds,   187
Let shame say what it will. When these are gone,
The woman will be out. Adieu, my lord!
I have a speech of fire, that fain would blaze,
But that this folly douts it.   *Exit.*
    King.   Let's follow, Gertrude.
How much I had to do to calm his rage!   192
Now fear I this will give it start again.
Therefore let's follow.   *Exeunt.*

170 liberal: *free-spoken*
172 coronet: *garlanded*
178 incapable: *having no understanding*
179 indu'd: *endowed with qualities fitting her*
187 trick: *hereditary trait*
189 woman; *cf. n.*
                             191 douts: *extinguishes*

[ACT FIFTH

SCENE FIRST.

A Churchyard near Elsinore]

Enter two Clowns.

[*First*] *Clo.* Is she to be buried in Christian burial when she wilfully seeks her own salvation?

Other. I tell thee she is. Therefore make her grave straight. The crowner hath sat on her and finds it Christian burial.   5

Clown. How can that be, unless she drowned herself in her own defence?

Other. Why, 'tis found so.

Clown. It must be *se offendendo*; it cannot be else. For here lies the point: if I drown myself wittingly, it argues an act, and an act hath three branches; it is to act, to do, to perform. Argal, she drowned herself wittingly.

Other. Nay, but hear you, goodman delver,—   14

Clown. Give me leave. Here lies the water; good. Here stands the man; good. If the man go to this water and drown himself, it is, will he, nill he, he goes; mark you that! But if the water come to him

S. d. Clowns; *cf. n.*
4 straight: *at once*   crowner: *coroner*   sat on: *passed on*
9 *se offendendo; cf. n.*   11 branches: *divisions*
12 Argal: *corruption of ergo, therefore*
14 goodman delver: *Mr. Sexton*

and drown him, he drowns not himself. Argal, he
that is not guilty of his own death shortens not his
own life.   21

Other. But is this law?

Clown. Ay, marry, is 't; crowner's quest law.   23

Other. Will you ha' the truth on 't? If this had not
been a gentlewoman, she should have been buried
out o' Christian burial.   26

Clown. Why, there thou sayest; and the more pity
that great folk should have countenance in this world
to drown or hang themselves more than their even
Christen. Come, my spade! There is no ancient
gentlemen but gardeners, ditchers, and grave-makers.
They hold up Adam's profession.   32

Other. Was he a gentleman?

Clown. 'A was the first that ever bore arms.

⟨*Other*. Why, he had none.   35

Clown. What! art a heathen? How dost thou understand the Scripture? The Scripture says, Adam
digged; could he dig without arms?⟩ I'll put another
question to thee. If thou answerest me not to the
purpose, confess thyself—

Other. Go to.   41

Clown. What is he that builds stronger than either
the mason, the shipwright, or the carpenter?

Other. The gallows-maker; for that frame outlives
a thousand tenants.   45

Clown. I like thy wit well. In good faith the gallows does well, but how does it well? It does well to

23 quest: *inquest*   29 even Christen: *fellow Christian*
34 bore arms; *cf. n.*   35–38 *not in Quarto*
40 confess thyself; *cf. n.*   41 Go to: *out with it!*

those that do ill. Now thou dost ill to say the gallows
is built stronger than the church. Argal, the gallows
may do well to thee. To 't again; come!

Other. Who builds stronger than a mason, a shipwright, or a carpenter?　　　　　　　　　　　　　52

Clown. Ay, tell me that, and unyoke.

Other. Marry, now I can tell.

Clown. To 't.

Other. Mass, I cannot tell.　　　　　　　　　　56

Enter Hamlet and Horatio afar off.

Clown. Cudgel thy brains no more about it, for
your dull ass will not mend his pace with beating;
and when you are asked this question next, say, 'a
grave-maker.' The houses he makes lasts till doomsday. Go, get thee to Yaughan and fetch me a stoup
of liquor.　　　　　　　　　　[*Exit other Clown.*]

[Clown digs and] sings.

In youth, when I did love, did love,　　　　　　63
　　Methought it was very sweet.
To contract—oh—the time, for—ah—my behove,
　　O methought there—ah—was nothing—ah—meet.

Ham. Has this fellow no feeling of his business,
that he sings at grave-making?　　　　　　　　68

Hor. Custom hath made it in him a property of
easiness.

53 unyoke; *cf. n.*
61 Yaughan; *cf. n.*　　stoup: *two quart measure*
63 In . . . love; *cf. n.*
65 contract: *shorten (with pleasure)*　　behove: *benefit*
66 meet: *good enough*　　　　　69 property of easiness; *cf. n.*

Ham. 'Tis e'en so; the hand of little employment hath the daintier sense.   72

Clown. But age, with his stealing steps,   *Song.*
    Hath claw'd me in his clutch,
    And hath shipp'd me intil the land,
    As if I had never been such.   76

[*Throws up a skull.*]

Ham. That skull had a tongue in it and could sing once. How the knave jowls it to the ground, as if 't were Cain's jaw-bone, that did the first murther! This might be the pate of a politician which this ass now o'erreaches, one that would circumvent God, might it not?   82

Hor. It might, my lord.

Ham. Or of a courtier, which could say, 'Good morrow, sweet lord! How dost thou, good lord?' This might be my Lord Such-a-one, that praised my Lord Such-a-one's horse when 'a went to beg it, might it not?   88

Hor. Ay, my lord.

Ham. Why, e'en so, and now my Lady Worm's: chapless, and knocked about the mazzard with a sexton's spade. Here's fine revolution, an we had the trick to see 't. Did these bones cost no more the breeding but to play at loggats with 'em? Mine ache to think on 't.   95

72 sense: *sensibility*   75 intil: *into*   78 jowls: *dashes*
79 Cain's jaw-bone, that: *the jaw-bone of Cain, who; cf. n.*
81 o'erreaches; *cf. n.*
87 went: *went about, attempted; cf. n.*
91 chapless: *lacking the lower jaw*   mazzard: *head*
94 loggats; *cf. n.*

Clown. A pick-axe and a spade, a spade,   *Song.*
    For and a shrouding sheet;
  O, a pit of clay for to be made
    For such a guest is meet.

[*Throws up another skull.*]

Ham. There's another! Why may not that be the skull of a lawyer? Where be his quiddities now, his quillets, his cases, his tenures, and his tricks? Why does he suffer this rude knave now to knock him about the sconce with a dirty shovel, and will not tell him of his action of battery? Hum! This fellow might be in 's time a great buyer of land, with his statutes, his recognizances, his fines, his double vouchers, his recoveries. ⟨Is this the fine of his fines, and the recovery of his recoveries,⟩ to have his fine pate full of fine dirt? Will his vouchers vouch him no more of his purchases, and double ones too, than the length and breadth of a pair of indentures? The very conveyances of his lands will scarcely lie in this box, and must th' inheritor himself have no more, ha?

Hor. Not a jot more, my lord.   115

Ham. Is not parchment made of sheep skins?

Hor. Ay, my lord, and of calves' skins too.   117

Ham. They are sheep and calves which seek out assurance in that. I will speak to this fellow. Whose grave 's this, sirrah?

101 quiddities: *subtleties*
102 quillets: *minute distinctions*   tenures; *cf. n.*
104 sconce: *head*   105 action of battery; *cf. n.*
107 statutes; *cf. n.*   recognizances; *cf. n.*   fines; *cf. n.*
108 vouchers; *cf. n.*   recoveries; *cf. n.*   fine: *end*
108, 109 Is . . . recoveries; *not in Quarto*
112 indentures: *mutual agreements; cf. n.*
113 conveyances; *cf. n.*   119 assurance: *security; cf. n.*

Clown. Mine, sir,

> O, a pit of clay for to be made   122
>   For such a guest is meet.

Ham. I think it be thine indeed, for thou liest in 't.

Clown. You lie out on 't, sir, and therefore 't is not yours. For my part, I do not lie in 't, yet it is mine.   128

Ham. Thou dost lie in 't, to be in 't and say it is thine. 'Tis for the dead, not for the quick. Therefore thou liest.

Clown. 'Tis a quick lie, sir. 'Twill away again from me to you.

Ham. What man dost thou dig it for?   134

Clown. For no man, sir.

Ham. What woman, then?

Clown. For none, neither.

Ham. Who is to be buried in 't?   138

Clown. One that was a woman, sir; but, rest her soul, she's dead.

Ham. How absolute the knave is! we must speak by the card, or equivocation will undo us. By the Lord, Horatio, this three years I have took note of it; the age is grown so picked that the toe of the peasant comes so near the heel of the courtier he galls his kibe.—How long hast thou been grave-maker?   146

Clown. Of all the days i' th' year, I came to 't that day that our last King Hamlet overcame Fortinbras.

141 absolute: *precise*
142 by the card: *with precision; cf. n.*
144 picked: *fastidious; cf. n.*
146 kibe: *chilblain*

Ham. How long is that since?   149

Clown. Cannot you tell that? Every fool can tell that. It was that very day that young Hamlet was born,—he that is mad and sent into England.   152

Ham. Ay, marry! Why was he sent into England?

Clown. Why, because 'a was mad. 'A shall recover his wits there; or if 'a do not, 'tis no great matter there.   156

Ham. Why?

Clown. 'Twill not be seen in him there. There the men are as mad as he.   159

Ham. How came he mad?

Clown. Very strangely, they say.

Ham. How, strangely?   162

Clown. Faith, e'en with losing his wits.

Ham. Upon what ground?

Clown. Why, here in Denmark. I have been sexton here, man and boy, thirty years.   166

Ham. How long will a man lie i' th' earth ere he rot?

Clown. Faith, if 'a be not rotten before 'a die (as we have many pocky corses now-a-days, that will scarce hold the laying in) 'a will last you some eight year or nine year. A tanner will last you nine year.

Ham. Why he more than another?   173

Clown. Why, sir, his hide is so tanned with his trade that 'a will keep out water a great while, and your water is a sore decayer of your whoreson dead body. Here's a skull now hath lien you i' th' earth three-and-twenty years.   178

176 sore: *grievous*   whoreson: *plagued*
177 lien: *lain*   178 three-and-twenty years; *cf. n.*

Ham. Whose was it?

Clown. A whoreson mad fellow's it was. Whose do you think it was?

Ham. Nay, I know not.   182

Clown. A pestilence on him for a mad rogue! 'a poured a flagon of Rhenish on my head once. This same skull, sir, was Sir Yorick's skull, the king's jester.

Ham. This!

Clown. E'en that.   188

Ham. ⟨Let me see.⟩ [*Takes the skull.*]—Alas, poor Yorick! I knew him, Horatio; a fellow of infinite jest, of most excellent fancy. He hath bore me on his back a thousand times; and now, how abhorred in my imagination it is! my gorge rises at it. Here hung those lips that I have kissed I know not how oft. Where be your gibes now? your gambols? your songs? your flashes of merriment, that were wont to set the table on a roar? Not one now, to mock your own grinning; quite chapfallen. Now get you to my lady's chamber, and tell her, let her paint an inch thick, to this favor she must come. Make her laugh at that. Prithee, Horatio, tell me one thing.

Hor. What's that, my lord?   202

Ham. Dost thou think Alexander looked o' this fashion i' th' earth?

Hor. E'en so.

Ham. And smelt so? pah!   206

[*Puts down the skull.*]

Hor. E'en so, my lord.

Ham. To what base uses we may return, Horatio!
Why may not imagination trace the noble dust of
Alexander till 'a find it stopping a bunghole? 210

Hor. 'Twere to consider too curiously, to consider
so. *minutely*

Ham. No, faith, not a jot; but to follow him thither
with modesty enough, and likelihood to lead it; ⟨as
thus:⟩ Alexander died, Alexander was buried, Alexander returneth to dust; the dust is earth. Of earth
we make loam, and why of that loam, whereto he
was converted, might they not stop a beer-barrel?

Imperious Cæsar, dead and turn'd to clay,
Might stop a hole to keep the wind away. 220
O that that earth, which kept the world in awe,
Should patch a wall t' expel the winter's flaw!

But soft! but soft awhile! Here comes the king.

*Enter King, Queen, Laertes, [a Priest,] and a Coffin,
with Lords attendant.*

The queen, the courtiers! Who is this they follow? 224
And with such maimed rites? This doth betoken
The corse they follow did with desperate hand
Fordo it own life. 'Twas of some estate.
Couch we awhile, and mark. 228
[*Retires with Horatio.*]

Laer. What ceremony else?
Ham.   That is Laertes,
A very noble youth. Mark.

211 curiously: *minutely*
214 modesty: *moderation*   likelihood: *probability*
222 flaw: *squall of wind*   223 awhile; *cf. n.*
227 Fordo it: *undo its*   estate: *rank*
228 Couch: *remain concealed*

Laer. What ceremony else?

Priest. Her obsequies have been as far enlarg'd   232
As we have warranty. Her death was doubtful,
And but that great command o'ersways the order,
She should in ground unsanctified been lodg'd
Till the last trumpet; for charitable prayers,   236
Shards, flints, and pebbles should be thrown on her.
Yet here she is allow'd her virgin crants,
Her maiden strewments, and the bringing home
Of bell and burial.   240

Laer. Must there no more be done?

Priest.   No more be done.
We should profane the service of the dead
To sing a requiem and such rest to her
As to peace-parted souls.

Laer.   Lay her i' th' earth,   244
And from her fair and unpolluted flesh
May violets spring! I tell thee, churlish priest,
A ministering angel shall my sister be
When thou liest howling.

Ham.   What! the fair Ophelia?   248

Queen. [*Scattering flowers.*] Sweets to the sweet! fare-
    well!
I hop'd thou shouldst have been my Hamlet's wife.
I thought thy bride-bed to have deck'd, sweet maid,
And not have strew'd thy grave.

Laer.   O treble woe   252

232 enlarg'd: *extended*
233 warranty: *warrant*   doubtful: *suspicious*
234 Cf. *n.*   235 been: *have been; cf. n.*
237 Shards: *fragments of pottery*   238 crants: *garland; cf. n.*
239 strewments: *flowers strewn on a grave*
244 peace-parted: *piously deceased*

Seems ridiculous that Hamlet jumps in grave.

Fall ten times treble on that cursed head
Whose wicked deed thy most ingenious sense
Depriv'd thee of. Hold off the earth awhile,
Till I have caught her once more in mine arms.

        Leaps in the grave.

Now pile your dust upon the quick and dead,
Till of this flat a mountain you have made 258
T' o'er-top old Pelion or the skyish head
Of blue Olympus.

 Ham. [*Advancing.*] What is he whose grief
Bears such an emphasis? whose phrase of sorrow 261
Conjures the wandering stars, and makes them stand
Like wonder-wounded hearers? This is I,
Hamlet the Dane.   *Hamlet leaps in after Laertes.*

 Laer.   The devil take thy soul! 264

        [*Grapples with him.*]

 Ham. Thou pray'st not well.
I prithee take thy fingers from my throat;
For though I am not splenetive and rash,
Yet have I in me something dangerous, 268
Which let thy wisdom fear. Hold off thy hand!

 King. Pluck them asunder.

 Queen.   Hamlet! Hamlet!

 «*All.* Gentlemen!»

 Hor.   Good my lord, be quiet.

    [*The Attendants part them, and they come
       out of the grave.*]

 Ham. Why, I will fight with him upon this theme 272
Until my eyelids will no longer wag.

---

254 ingenious: *delicately sensitive*   259 Pelion; *cf. n.*
262 wandering stars: *planets* 264 Hamlet the Dane; *cf. n.*
267 splenetive: *quick-tempered*

Queen. O my son, what theme?

Ham. <u>I lov'd Ophelia. Forty thousand brothers</u>
<u>Could not with all their quantity of love</u>   276
<u>Make up my sum.</u> What wilt thou do for her?

King. O, he is mad, Laertes.

Queen. For love of God, forbear him.

Ham. 'Swounds, show me <u>what thou't do.</u>
<u>Woo't weep? woo't fight? «woo't fast?» woo't tear thy-</u>
    self?   281
<u>Woo't drink up eisel? eat a crocodile?</u>
<u>I'll do 't. Dost thou come here to whine?</u>
To outface me with leaping in her grave?   284
<u>Be buried quick with her, and so will I.</u>
And if thou prate of mountains, let them throw
Millions of acres on us, till our ground,
Singeing his pate against the burning zone,   288
Make Ossa like a wart! Nay, an thou'lt mouth,
I'll rant as well as thou.

Queen.   This is mere madness,
And thus a while the fit will work on him.
Anon, as patient as the female dove,   292
When that her golden couplets are disclos'd,
His silence will sit drooping.

Ham.   Hear you, sir.
What is the reason that you use me thus?
I lov'd you ever,—but it is no matter.   296
Let Hercules himself do what he may,
The cat will mew and dog will have his day.   *Exit.*

279 forbear him: *leave him alone*   281 Woo't: *wilt thou*
282 eisel: *vinegar (associated with gall)*
288 burning zone: *'coelum igneum,' heavenly region of fire*
293 golden couplets; *cf. n.*

King. I pray thee, good Horatio, wait upon him.

[*Exit Horatio.*]

[*To Laertes.*] Strengthen your patience in our last night's
  speech.   300
We'll put the matter to the present push.—
Good Gertrude, set some watch over your son.
This grave shall have a living monument.
An hour of quiet shortly shall we see;   304
Till then, in patience our proceeding be.   *Exeunt.*

[SCENE SECOND.

The Hall in the Castle]

Enter Hamlet and Horatio.

Ham. So much for this, sir; now shall you see the other.
You do remember all the circumstance?

Hor. Remember it, my lord!

Ham. Sir, in my heart there was a kind of fighting   4
That would not let me sleep. Methought I lay
Worse than the mutines in the bilboes. Rashly,—
And prais'd be rashness for it (let us know,
Our indiscretion sometimes serves us well   8
When our deep plots do pall; and that should learn us
There's a divinity that shapes our ends,
Rough-hew them how we will)—

Hor.   That is most certain.

Ham. Up from my cabin,   12

300 in: *in the thought of*
301 present push: *immediate trial*   303 living: *lasting*
6 mutines: *mutineers*   bilboes: *shackles*   9 pall: *fail*

My sea-gown scarf'd about me, in the dark
Grop'd I to find out them, had my desire,
Finger'd their packet, and in fine withdrew
To mine own room again; making so bold   16
(My fears forgetting manners) to unseal
Their grand commission, where I found, Horatio,
(Ah, royal knavery!) an exact command,—
Larded with many several sorts of reasons   20
Importing Denmark's health and England's too,
With, ho! such bugs and goblins in my life,—
That, on the supervise, no leisure bated,
No, not to stay the grinding of the axe,   24
My head should be struck off.

    Hor.   Is 't possible?

    Ham. Here's the commission: read it at more leisure.
But wilt thou hear now how I did proceed?

    Hor. I beseech you.   28

    Ham. Being thus be-netted round with villainies,
Ere I could make a prologue to my brains
They had begun the play. I sat me down,
Devis'd a new commission, wrote it fair.—   32
I once did hold it, as our statists do,
A baseness to write fair and labor'd much
How to forget that learning, but, sir, now
It did me yeoman's service. Wilt thou know   36
Th' effect of what I wrote?

13 sea-gown; *cf. n.*   15 Finger'd: *pilfered*
22 bugs . . . life; *cf. n.*
23 supervise: *perusal*   bated: *deducted*
29 be-netted: *ensnared*   30 prologue . . . play; *cf. n.*
33 statists: *statesmen*
36 yeoman's service: *good and faithful service*

Hor.   Ay, good my lord.

Ham. An earnest conjuration from the king,
As England was his faithful tributary,
As love between them like the palm might flourish,   40
As peace should still her wheaten garland wear
And stand a comma 'tween their amities,
And many such-like 'As'es of great charge,
That, on the view and knowing of these contents,   44
Without debatement further, more or less,
He should those bearers put to sudden death,
Not shriving-time allow'd.

Hor.   How was this seal'd?

Ham. Why, even in that was heaven ordinant.   48
I had my father's signet in my purse,
Which was the model of that Danish seal.—
Folded the writ up in the form of th' other,
Subscrib'd it, gave 't th' impression, plac'd it safely,   52
The changeling never known. Now, the next day
Was our sea-fight, and what to this was sequent
Thou know'st already.

Hor. So Guildenstern and Rosencrantz go to 't.   56

Ham. ⟨Why, man, they did make love to this employ-
ment;⟩
They are not near my conscience. Their defeat
Does by their own insinuation grow.

---

41 wheaten garland: *emblem of peace*
42 comma: *bond of connection; cf. n.*   43 'As'es; *cf. n.*
47 shriving-time: *time for absolution*
48 ordinant: *controlling*   50 model: *exact likeness*
52 Subscrib'd: *signed*   impression: *i.e., of the seal*
53 changeling: *substitute*
57, 68–80 *not in Quarto*   59 insinuation: *intrusion*

'Tis dangerous when the baser nature comes   60
Between the pass and fell-incensed points
Of mighty opposites.
     Hor.   Why, what a king is this!
     Ham. Does it not, think thee, stand me now upon?
He that hath kill'd my king and whor'd my mother,   64
Popp'd in between th' election and my hopes,
Thrown out his angle for my proper life,
And with such cozenage—is 't not perfect conscience
⟨To quit him with this arm? and is 't not to be damn'd
To let this canker of our nature come   69
In further evil?
     Hor. It must be shortly known to him from England
What is the issue of the business there.   72
     Ham. It will be short. The interim is mine,
And a man's life's no more than to say 'One.'
But I am very sorry, good Horatio,
That to Laertes I forgot myself,   76
For by the image of my cause I see
The portraiture of his. I'll court his favors:
But sure the bravery of his grief did put me
Into a towering passion.
     Hor.   Peace! who comes here?⟩   80

                    Enter young Osric.
     Osr. Your lordship is right welcome back to Den-
mark.

61 fell-incensed: *cruelly angered; cf. n.*
62 opposites: *opponents*
63 stand . . . upon: *vitally concern*
65 election; *cf. n.*   66 angle: *fishing-hook*   proper: *own*
67 cozenage: *cheating*   79 bravery: *ostentatious display*

Ham. I humbly thank you, sir. [*Aside to Horatio.*]
Dost know this water-fly?   84

Hor. [*Aside to Hamlet.*] No, my good lord.

Ham. [*Aside to Horatio.*] Thy state is the more
gracious, for 'tis a vice to know him. He hath much
land, and fertile. Let a beast be lord of beasts, and his
crib shall stand at the king's mess. 'Tis a chough, but,
as I say, spacious in the possession of dirt.   90

Osr. Sweet lord, if your lordship were at leisure, I
should impart a thing to you from his majesty.

Ham. I will receive it, sir, with all diligence of
spirit. Put your bonnet to his right use; 'tis for the
head.   95

Osr. I thank your lordship. It is very hot.

Ham. No, believe me, 'tis very cold; the wind is
northerly.   98

Osr. It is indifferent cold, my lord, indeed.

Ham. But yet methinks it is very sultry and hot for
my complexion.   101

Osr. Exceedingly, my lord. It is very sultry, as
'twere,—I cannot tell how. But, my lord, his majesty
bade me signify to you that 'a has laid a great wager
on your head. Sir, this is the matter,—   105

Ham. I beseech you, remember—

                    [*Hamlet moves him to put on his hat.*]

Osr. Nay, good my lord, for my ease, in good
faith. «Sir, here is newly come to court Laertes,—
believe me, an absolute gentleman, full of most excel-

84 water-fly; *cf. n.*
89 mess; *cf. n.*   chough: *small chattering bird*
106 remember; *cf. n.*   107 my ease; *cf. n.*
108–137 *not in Folio*   109 absolute: *perfect*

lent differences, of very soft society and great showing. Indeed, to speak feelingly of him, he is the card
or calendar of gentry, for you shall find in him the
continent of what part a gentleman would see.   113

Ham. Sir, his definement suffers no perdition in
you; though, I know, to divide him inventorially
would dozy th' arithmetic of memory, and yet but
yaw neither, in respect of his quick sail. But, in the
verity of extolment, I take him to be a soul of great
article, and his infusion of such dearth and rareness
as, to make true diction of him, his semblable is his
mirror, and who else would trace him his umbrage,
nothing more.   122

Osr. Your lordship speaks most infallibly of him.

Ham. The concernancy, sir? why do we wrap the
gentleman in our more rawer breath?

Osr. Sir?

Hor. Is 't not possible to understand in another
tongue? You will to 't, sir, really.   128

Ham. What imports the nomination of this gentleman?

Osr. Of Laertes?   131

110 differences: *distinguishing features*   soft: *gentle*
111 card: *map*
114 definement: *description*   perdition: *loss*
115 divide inventorially: *catalogue*   116 dozy: *make giddy*
117 yaw: *stagger; cf. n.*   neither: *too*
119 great article: *large scope*   infusion: *character imparted by nature*
120 semblable: *like*   121 trace: *follow*   umbrage: *shadow*
124 concernancy: *relevance*   125 more rawer: *too unskilled*
127 another tongue; *cf. n.*
128 You will to 't: *You will acquire the art*
129 nomination: *naming*

Hor. His purse is empty already. All 's golden words are spent.

Ham. Of him, sir.

Osr. I know you are not ignorant—   135

Ham. I would you did, sir; yet in faith, if you did, it would not much approve me. Well, sir.»

Osr. You are not ignorant of what excellence Laertes is—

«*Ham.* I dare not confess that, lest I should compare with him in excellence; but to know a man well were to know himself.   142

Osr. I mean, sir,» for his weapon; «but in the imputation laid on him by them, in his meed he's unfellowed.»

Ham. What's his weapon?

Osr. Rapier and dagger.   147

Ham. That's two of his weapons, but,—well.

Osr. The king, sir, hath wagered with him six Barbary horses, against the which he has impawned, as I take it, six French rapiers and poniards, with their assigns; as girdle, hanger, and so. Three of the carriages, in faith, are very dear to fancy, very responsive to the hilts, most delicate carriages and of very liberal conceit.   155

137 approve me: *commend me*   140–145 *not in Folio*
140 compare with: *vie with*
144 imputation: *reputation*   meed: *merit, worth*   unfellowed: *without an equal*
150 impawned: *staked*
152 assigns: *appurtenances*   hanger: *strap from which a sword is suspended*
153 carriages: *hangers*   dear to fancy: *unusual in design*
154 delicate: *finely wrought* 155 liberal conceit: *tasteful design*

Ham. What call you the carriages?

«*Hor.* I knew you must be edified by the margent, ere you had done.»

Osr. The carriages, sir, are the hangers.   159

Ham. The phrase would be more germane to the matter, if we could carry a cannon by our sides. I would it might be hangers till then. But, on; six Barbary horses against six French swords, their assigns, and three liberal-conceited carriages; that's the French bet against the Danish. Why is this all impawned, as you call it?

Osr. The king, sir, hath laid that in a dozen passes between yourself and him, he shall not exceed you three hits. He hath laid on twelve for nine, and it would come to immediate trial, if your lordship would vouchsafe the answer.   171

Ham. How if I answer no?

Osr. I mean, my lord, the opposition of your person in trial.

Ham. Sir, I will walk here in the hall. If it please his majesty, it is the breathing time of day with me. Let the foils be brought, the gentleman willing, and the king hold his purpose, I will win for him an I can; if not, I will gain nothing but my shame and the odd hits.   180

Osr. Shall I deliver you so?

Ham. To this effect, sir, after what flourish your nature will.   183

Osr. I commend my duty to your lordship.

157–158 *not in Folio*   157 margent; *cf. n.*
169 twelve for nine; *cf. n.*
176 breathing time: *exercise period*

Ham. Yours, yours. [*Exit Osric.*] He does well to commend it himself; there are no tongues else for 's turn. 187

Hor. This lapwing runs away with the shell on his head.

Ham. 'A did comply, sir, with his dug before 'a sucked it. Thus has he—and many more of the same bevy, that I know the drossy age dotes on—only got the tune of the time and outward habit of encounter, a kind of yesty collection which carries them through and through the most fond and winnowed opinions; and do but blow them to their trial, the bubbles are out. 197

«Enter a Lord.

Lord. My lord, his majesty commended him to you by young Osric, who brings back to him that you attend him in the hall. He sends to know if your pleasure hold to play with Laertes, or that you will take longer time. 202

Ham. I am constant to my purposes; they follow the king's pleasure. If his fitness speaks, mine is ready, now or whensoever, provided I be so able as now.

Lord. The king and queen and all are coming down. 208

188 lapwing: *plover, a vivacious little bird* with . . . head: *almost before he is hatched*
190 comply: *use fine language*
192 drossy: *frivolous*
193 tune: *mood* outward . . . encounter: *superficial mannerisms*
194 yesty: *frothy*
195 fond and winnowed; *cf. n.* 197–212 *not in Folio*

Ham. In happy time.

Lord. The queen desires you to use some gentle
entertainment to Laertes before you fall to play.   211

Ham. She well instructs me.   [*Exit Lord.*]»

Hor. You will lose this wager, my lord.

Ham. I do not think so. Since he went into France,
I have been in continual practice. I shall win at the
odds, but thou wouldst not think how ill all 's here
about my heart. But it is no matter.   217

Hor. Nay, good my lord,—

Ham. It is but foolery, but it is such a kind of gaingiving as would perhaps trouble a woman.   220

Hor. If your mind dislike anything, obey it. I will
forestall their repair hither and say you are not fit.   222

Ham. Not a whit, we defy augury; there is special
providence in the fall of a sparrow. If it be now, 'tis
not to come; if it be not to come, it will be now; if
it be not now, yet it will come: the readiness is all.
Since no man has aught of what he leaves, what is 't
to leave betimes? «Let be.»   228

*Enter King, Queen, Laertes and Lords, with other At-
tendants with foils and gauntlets. A table and flagons
of wine on it.*

King. Come, Hamlet, come, and take this hand from
me.

[*The King puts the hand of Laertes into
that of Hamlet.*]

Ham. Give me your pardon, sir. I've done you wrong;
But pardon 't, as you are a gentleman.

This presence knows, and you must needs have heard,

209 In happy time: *at an appropriate time*
219 gaingiving: *foreboding*   232 presence: *royal assembly*

How I am punish'd with a sore distraction.
What I have done,   234
That might your nature, honor, and exception
Roughly awake, I here proclaim was madness.
Was 't Hamlet wrong'd Laertes? Never Hamlet.
If Hamlet from himself be ta'en away,   238
And when he's not himself does wrong Laertes,
Then Hamlet does it not; Hamlet denies it.
Who does it then? His madness. If 't be so,
Hamlet is of the faction that is wrong'd;   242
His madness is poor Hamlet's enemy.
⟨Sir, in this audience,⟩
Let my disclaiming from a purpos'd evil
Free me so far in your most generous thoughts,
That I have shot my arrow o'er the house,   247
And hurt my brother.
    Laer.   I am satisfied in nature,
Whose motive in this case should stir me most
To my revenge; but in my terms of honor   250
I stand aloof, and will no reconcilement
Till by some elder masters of known honor
I have a voice and precedent of peace,
To keep my name ungor'd. But till that time,
I do receive your offer'd love like love,   255
And will not wrong it.
    Ham.   I embrace it freely,
And will this brothers' wager frankly play.
Give us the foils. ⟨Come on.⟩
    Laer.   Come, one for me.   258

235 exception: *disapproval*   244 *Not in Quarto*
248 satisfied in nature; *cf. n.*
253 voice: *opinion*   254 ungor'd: *uninjured*

Ham. I'll be your foil, Laertes. In mine ignorance
Your skill shall, like a star i' th' darkest night,
Stick fiery off indeed.

 Laer.   You mock me, sir.

 Ham. No, by this hand.   262

 King. Give them the foils, young Osric. Cousin Hamlet,
You know the wager?

 Ham.   Very well, my lord;
Your Grace has laid the odds o' th' weaker side.

 King. I do not fear it. I have seen you both;
But since he is better'd, we have therefore odds.

 Laer. This is too heavy; let me see another.

 Ham. This likes me well. These foils have all a length?

 Osr. Ay, my good lord.   270

          Prepare to play.

 King. Set me the stoups of wine upon that table.
If Hamlet give the first or second hit,
Or quit in answer of the third exchange,
Let all the battlements their ordnance fire. 274
The king shall drink to Hamlet's better breath;
And in the cup an union shall he throw,
Richer than that which four successive kings
In Denmark's crown have worn. Give me the cups; 278
And let the kettle to the trumpet speak,
The trumpet to the cannoneer without,
The cannons to the heavens, the heaven to earth:
'Now the king drinks to Hamlet!'   *Trumpets*
    Come, begin!   *the while.*

---

259 foil; *cf. n.*   261 Stick . . . off: *stand out in relief*
273 quit; *cf. n.*
276 union: *pearl*
          279 kettle: *kettledrum*

And you, the judges, bear a wary eye.   283

   Ham. Come on, sir.

   Laer.   Come, my lord.   *They play.*

   Ham.   One.

   Laer.   No.

   Ham.   Judgment.

   Osr. A hit, a very palpable hit.

                   «*Drum, trumpets and shot.*
                   Flourish. A piece goes off.»

   Laer.   Well; again.

   King. Stay; give me drink. Hamlet, this pearl is thine.
Here's to thy health. Give him the cup.   287

            ⟨*Trumpets sound; and shot goes off.*⟩

   Ham. I'll play this bout first; set it by awhile.
Come.—[*They play.*] Another hit! What say you?

   Laer. ⟨A touch, a touch,⟩ I do confess 't.   290

   King. Our son shall win.

   Queen.   He's fat and scant of breath.
Here, Hamlet, take my napkin, rub thy brows.
The queen carouses to thy fortune, Hamlet.

                   [*Takes Hamlet's cup.*]

   Ham. Good madam!

   King.   Gertrude, do not drink!   294

   Queen. I will, my lord; I pray you, pardon me.

   King. [*Aside.*] It is the poison'd cup! it is too late.

   Ham. I dare not drink yet, madam. By and by.

   Queen. Come, let me wipe thy face.   298

   Laer. My lord, I'll hit him now.

   King.   I do not think 't.

   Laer. [*Aside.*] And yet it is almost against my con-
    science.

291 fat: *out of training*   292 napkin: *handkerchief*

Ham. Come, for the third! Laertes, you but dally;
I pray you, pass with your best violence.   302
I am afeard you make a wanton of me.

    Laer. Say you so? come on.   *Play.*

    Osr. Nothing, neither way.

    Laer. Have at you now.

                In scuffling they change rapiers.

    King.   Part them! they are incens'd.

    Ham. Nay, come again!   [*The Queen falls.*]

    Osr.   Look to the queen there. Ho!

    Hor. They bleed on both sides. How is it, my lord?

    Osr. How is 't, Laertes?

    Laer. Why, as a woodcock to mine own springe,
    Osric.   ·   310
I am justly kill'd with mine own treachery.

    Ham. How does the queen?

    King.   She sounds to see them bleed.

    Queen. No, no, the drink, the drink! O my dear Ham-
    let!   313
The drink, the drink! I am poison'd.   [*Dies.*]

    Ham. O villainy! Ho! let the door be lock'd.
Treachery! seek it out.   [*Laertes falls.*]

    Laer. It is here, Hamlet. Hamlet, thou art slain;
No medicine in the world can do thee good.   318
In thee there is not half an hour's life.
The treacherous instrument is in thy hand,
Unbated and envenom'd. The foul practice
Hath turn'd itself on me. Lo, here I lie,   322
Never to rise again. Thy mother's poison'd.
I can no more. The king, the king's to blame.

302 pass: *thrust*   303 wanton: *pampered child*
306 S. d. *Cf. n.*   312 sounds: *swoons*

Ham. The point envenom'd too?
Then, venom, to thy work!   *Hurts the King.*
    All.   Treason! treason!   326
    King. O yet defend me, friends; I am but hurt.
    Ham. Here, thou incestuous, murd'rous, damned Dane,
Drink off this potion! Is thy union here?   329
Follow my mother.   *King dies.*
    Laer.   He is justly serv'd;
It is a poison temper'd by himself.
Exchange forgiveness with me, noble Hamlet:
Mine and my father's death come not upon thee,
Nor thine on me!   *Dies.*
    Ham. Heaven make thee free of it! I follow thee.   335
I am dead, Horatio. Wretched queen, adieu!
You that look pale and tremble at this chance,
That are but mutes or audience to this act,   338
Had I but time (as this fell sergeant, death,
Is strict in his arrest) O, I could tell you—
But let it be. Horatio, I am dead;   341
Thou liv'st. Report me and my cause aright
To the unsatisfied.
    Hor.   Never believe it!
I am more an antique Roman than a Dane.
Here's yet some liquor left.
    Ham.   As th' art a man,   345
Give me the cup! let go! by heaven, I'll have 't!
O good Horatio, what a wounded name
(Things standing thus unknown) shall live behind me.
If thou didst ever hold me in thy heart,   349
Absent thee from felicity awhile,

331 temper'd: *compounded*
339 sergeant: *sheriff's officer*   344 Roman; *cf. n.*

And in this harsh world draw thy breath in pain,
To tell my story.

> *A march afar off ⟨and shout within⟩*
>
> What warlike noise is this?

Enter Osric.

Osr. Young Fortinbras, with conquest come from Po-
　　land,　　　　　　　　　　　　　　　　　　　353
To the ambassadors of England gives
This warlike volley.

Ham.　　　　　　　O, I die, Horatio;
The potent poison quite o'er-crows my spirit.
I cannot live to hear the news from England,　　357
But I do prophesy th' election lights
On Fortinbras. He has my dying voice.
So tell him, with th' occurrents, more and less,
Which have solicited—The rest is silence.　　*Dies.*

Hor. Now cracks a noble heart. Good night, sweet
　　prince,—　　　　　　　　　　　　　　　　362
And flights of angels sing thee to thy rest!
Why does the drum come hither?

> *Enter Fortinbras, and English Ambassador, with
> drum, colors, and Attendants.*

Fort. Where is this sight?

Hor.　　　　　　　What is it you would see?　365
If aught of woe or wonder, cease your search.

Fort. This quarry cries on havoc. O proud death,

355 This warlike volley; *cf. n.*
356 o'er-crows: *triumphs over*　　　360 occurrents: *incidents*
361 solicited: *moved; cf. n.*　　　　363 flights: *troops*
367 quarry: *heap of slain*　　cries on havoc: *proclaims merciless*
　　slaughter; cf. n.

What feast is toward in thine eternal cell,
That thou so many princes at a shot   369
So bloodily hast struck?

   Amb.   The sight is dismal,
And our affairs from England come too late.
The ears are senseless that should give us hearing,
To tell him his commandment is fulfill'd,   373
That Rosencrantz and Guildenstern are dead.
Where should we have our thanks?

   Hor.   Not from his mouth,
Had it th' ability of life to thank you.   376
He never gave commandment for their death.
But since, so jump upon this bloody question,
You from the Polack wars, and you from England,
Are here arriv'd, give order that these bodies
High on a stage be placed to the view;   381
And let me speak to th' yet unknowing world
How these things came about. So shall you hear
Of carnal, bloody, and unnatural acts,
Of accidental judgments, casual slaughters,   385
Of deaths put on by cunning and forc'd cause,
And, in this upshot, purposes mistook
Fall'n on th' inventors' heads. All this can I
Truly deliver.

   Fort.   Let us haste to hear it,   389
And call the noblest to the audience.
For me, with sorrow I embrace my fortune.
I have some rights of memory in this kingdom,
Which now to claim my vantage doth invite me.   393

   Hor. Of that I shall have also cause to speak,

---

381 stage: *platform*   385 casual: *unpremeditated*
386 forc'd: *unreal*   392 rights of memory: *ancient claims*

And from his mouth whose voice will draw on more.
But let this same be presently perform'd,
Even while men's minds are wild, lest more mischance
On plots and errors happen.

  Fort.   Let four captains 398
Bear Hamlet like a soldier to the stage;
For he was likely, had he been put on,
To have prov'd most royal. And for his passage
The soldiers' music and the rites of war 402
Speak loudly for him!
Take up the bodies. Such a sight as this
Becomes the field, but here shows much amiss.
Go bid the soldiers shoot. 406

    Exeunt ⟨*marching, after the which a peal of*
        ordnance are shot off⟩.

395 draw on more: *be seconded by others*
400 been put on: *been put to the proof, tried*
401 royal; *cf. n.*   403 Speak; *cf. n.*

FINIS

NOTES

At the time of his sudden death in June of 1946, Professor Brooke had completed his work on the text, notes, and glosses for Hamlet, King Lear, Othello and I Henry IV. The editorial tasks which he left unfinished—preparation of some of the final copy for the press, reading of the proofs, compilation of the Indexes of Words Glossed, decisions as to certain matters of style and format, and, in the case of ' Henry IV, the rescuing of the text from the prescriptive punctuation of the eighteenth-century editors—have been undertaken by Professor Benjamin Nangle.

TEXTUAL NOTE. The two authorities for the text of *Hamlet* are the second quarto (separate) edition of the play published in 1604–05 and the version included in the first folio (collected) edition of Shakespeare's dramatic works, published in 1623. The Quarto text, though marred by bad typographical errors, is fundamentally the more reliable, and is usually (but by no means always) to be preferred. In the present book matter which the Folio omits is set within ornamental brackets (« »). This mainly represents cuts made in the stage version of the play as acted in Shakespeare's time. Matter which the Quarto omits is set within angle brackets (⟨ ⟩). This is largely material excised because indiscreet in 1604 or over-topical.

The bad First Quarto of the play, printed in 1603, is untrustworthy, but is occasionally of use in explaining doubtful passages or illustrating early stage practice.

The stage directions here reprinted are those of the Second Quarto, the Folio, and very occasionally of the First Quarto. Necessary amplifications and other essential matter omitted in the original editions are supplied within square brackets ([ ]). The early quartos do not divide the play into acts or scenes. Such a division was attempted in the First Folio and was carried out, with some incompleteness and with Latin headings ('Actus Primus. Scaena Prima,' *etc.*) through the first two acts. The act and scene division in the last three acts, and all indications of the place of action, are the work of post-Shakespearean editors, beginning with the Betterton acting text of 1676.

In Shakespeare's usage it was optional to give full syllabic value to the ending *-ed* of past verbal forms or (as is usually done now) to contract this ending with the preceding syllable. In the present text final *-ed* must always be pronounced as a separate syllable in order to preserve the original rhythm of the verse. Where rhythm requires the contracted form, the spelling *-'d* is used.

Shakespeare accented a number of words on syllables which now do not bear the accent, and sometimes his practice in this matter was inconsistent. Where an unusual accentuation is required, it is indicated by an acute mark over the stressed vowel, as in *canóniz'd*.

Obsolete words and words used in now unusual senses are explained in footnotes the first time they appear in the text. Repetitions are not noted and when they occur should be checked by the Index of Words Glossed at the end of the volume.

The critical and general notes in the present section are announced by the symbol, *cf. n.* ('confer notam'), at the bottom of the page of text to which each has reference. Names in parentheses at the end of notes indicate the authority for the information. No effort has been made to give precise credit either for information that has become common property or for that which, so far as known, is new in the present edition.

The Actors' Names. The first list of *dramatis personae* is found in the edition of 1676, which indicates the roles assumed by the actors of Thomas Betterton's company during Restoration performances of the play.

I.i.s.d. *Enter Bernardo and Francisco.* That is, they meet as the scene opens. The early editions regularly spell 'Barnardo,' which represents the Elizabethan pronunciation of the name.

I.i.3. *Long . . . king!* The pass-word or reply to the sentry's challenge.

I.i.15. *Friends . . . Dane.* When challenged by Francisco (who is now off duty) Horatio and Marcellus reply 'Friends' and 'Countrymen,' and are not asked for the pass-word. Like *Denmark* in line 48 below and *Dane* in line 44 of the next scene, *Dane* here means the king of Denmark.

I.i.19. *piece.* A humorous expression equivalent to 'something like him.'

I.i.37. *his.* Regularly used for 'its.' The latter form had not yet come into common use.

I.i.42. *scholar.* Scholars (and particularly scholars of Dr. Faustus' university, Wittenberg) had special competence to deal with spirits.

I.i.45. *It . . . to.* It was believed that a ghost could not speak until spoken to.

I.i.63. *sleaded pole-axe.* The first two Quartos agree in spelling 'sleaded pollax'; the Folio has 'sledded Pollax.' There seems to be no allusion to the Poles or 'Polacks' mentioned later in the play, though the Folio compositor may have thought so.

I.i.70. *Good now.* Interjectional expression denoting entreaty.

I.i.87. *law and heraldry.* The forms of both the common law and the law of arms having been duly observed. Nobles who signed binding agreements were wont to attach heraldic seals.

I.i.89. *lands . . . seiz'd of.* What Fortinbras staked was not his kingdom, but his personal landed possessions.

I.i.93. *cov'nant.* The Folio reading. Q2 has 'comart,' probably a misreading of Shakespeare's handwriting.

I.i.98. *list.* Literally, a special catalogue of the soldiers of a force; here used in the sense of an indiscriminately chosen crowd.

I.i.100. *hath a stomach.* I.e., gives an opportunity for courage. With a quibble on the literal meaning.

I.i.116+. The Quarto compositor (our only authority here) seems to have inadvertently skipped a line, perhaps because it began in the same way as 117. The line here conjecturally substituted is based upon the passage Shakespeare was remembering, where Plutarch writes (in North's translation) 'concerning the fires in the element [*i.e.*, sky] and spirits running up and down in the night' before Cæsar's death.

I.i.120. *sick . . . doomsday*. Perhaps a reference to the Biblical account in Matthew 24. 29: 'Immediately after the tribulation of those days shall the sun be darkened, and the moon shall not give her light.'

I.i.121. *fear'd*. The Quarto has 'feare.' Final 'e' and 'd' were often indistinguishable in Elizabethan handwriting.

I.i.125. *climatures*. A rare derivative from 'climate,' here meaning about as much as 'latitudes.' The passage is an echo of *Julius Cæsar*, I.iii.71–2, where Casca says of the omens:

> 'For I believe they are portentous things
> Unto the climate that they point upon.'

I.i.136. *uphoarded*. If while alive a person had hidden gold and placed it under a charm, it was necessary, for his soul's quiet, to release it from the spell. (Illustrated by Steevens from Dekker's *Knight's Conjuring*, 1607.)

I.i.140. *partisan*. A long-handled spear with a blade having one or more lateral cutting projections.

I.i.150. *cock*. It was a tradition that at cockcrow spirits returned to their confines.

I.i.157–164. This beautiful passage of (apparently unrecorded) folklore, preserved in the bad first Quarto as well as in the two good texts, is quite irrelevant to the business of the scene. It is clearly not Christmas at Elsinore and the spirits do stir abroad. Perhaps Shakespeare wrote it in anticipation of a Christmas court performance of the play, at which it would have been both appropriate and reassuring to the audience.

I.i.162. *planets strike*. The malignant aspects of planets, according to the pseudo-science of astrology, were supposed to be able to injure incautious travellers by night.

I.ii.s.d. *cum aliis*. With such other characters as the theatre manager may think proper (an author's note). The same vague phrase occurs in II.ii.s.d. This stage direction, following that in Q2, seems to define the scene as a meeting of the new king and queen with an administrative board similar to the Elizabethan Privy Council (Dover Wilson). The business transacted is suitable to such a meeting.

I.ii.65. *kin . . . kind*. I.e., more than his actual kinship and less than a natural relation. 'Kind' is here used equivocally for 'natural' and also for 'affectionate.' A proverbial expression occurring elsewhere in Elizabethan literature.

I.ii.67. *i' th' sun*. Probably Hamlet means he is too much in the unwelcome sunshine of the King's favor. The reply is purposely enigmatical. There is a quibble on 'sun' and 'son.'

I.ii.112. *importune*. The early editions agree in reading *impart toward(s)*; but to impart toward a person with nobility of love has never been intelligible English and the passage has never been adequately explained. The emendation suggested is, graphically, not unlikely. Shakespeare seems to have been prone to improperly doubled consonants. In the *Sonnets* (set up from his autograph probably) one finds such spellings as 'crittick,' 'pittifull,' 'widdowed,' 'boddies,' 'immitated,' *etc.* If he wrote 'importtune' here, it could have been very easily read as 'impart tow'd.' For the phrase 'importune with love' compare the next scene, line 110.

I.ii.113. *Wittenberg*. A famous German university, founded in 1502.

I.ii.140. *Hyperion*. The Titanic sun god, but here used for Apollo.

I.ii.149. *Niobe*. A daughter of Tantalus, who boasted that she had more sons and daughters than Leto. Consequently Apollo and Artemis slew her children with arrows, and she herself was turned by Zeus into a stone upon Mount Sipylus in Lydia, where she shed tears all the summer long.

I.ii.161. *forget myself*. *I.e.*, or I have lost the knowledge even of myself.

I.ii.175. *to drink deep*. The Second Quarto reading, 'for to drink,' may well be what Shakespeare wrote.

I.ii.180. *bak'd meats*. It was an old custom to have a feast as part of the funeral ceremonies.

I.ii.198. *waste*. It here means emptiness, the time when no living thing was seen.

I.ii.216. *it head*. The neuter possessive, *it,* is not infrequent in Shakespeare, doubtless to avoid the ambiguity of *his*. See note on I.i.37.

I.iii.7. *violet*. Early violets were proverbial examples of transitory things.

I.iii.26. *place*. Instead of *particular act and place* the Folio reads 'peculiar Sect and force.'

I.iii.53. *double blessing*. *I.e.*, because Laertes had already taken leave of his father and received his blessing.

I.iii.56. *wind . . . in the shoulder of*. Wind blowing from a stern quarter, hence 'behind,' 'favorable.'

I.iii.58. *precepts*. Many parallels for several of these precepts have been discovered. The most striking are Lord Burghley's instructions to his son, Robert Cecil (printed in J. Strype, *Annals of the Reformation, etc.*, 1824, IV, pp. 475–479).

I.iii.74. *clef.* That is, the best bred Frenchmen are noted for striking the perfect tone in dress. Shakespeare uses the word twice elsewhere, spelling it 'cliff.' The early texts virtually agree in misprinting the line: 'Are (Q2 Or) of a most select and generous (Q1 generall) chiefe (F cheff) in that.' It has long been regarded as a puzzle.

I.iii.99. *tenders.* Polonius, in l. 106, uses 'tenders' in the sense of promises to pay, which, as he says, are not legal currency. In line 107 the word means 'value' and in line 109 *tender me* may mean 'present me with' or 'exhibit yourself as'; but by that time Polonius has lost control of the word.

I.iii.109. *Running.* The figure is that of making a horse broken-winded by over-riding. The word is the happy guess of nine-teenth-century editors, Dyce and Collier. The Quarto reads 'Wrong' and the Folio 'Roaming.' (In Elizabethan handwriting 'w' may look very much like 'ru.')

I.iii.115. *woodcocks.* The woodcock was supposed to be a witless bird easily snared.

I.iii.130. *bawds.* One of the famous emendations of Lewis Theobald (1688–1744); 'bonds' in the original texts.

I.iv.33. *His.* So the text reads and it requires no change. Hamlet's attention turns from the group (*these men*, l. 30) to the typical individual.

I.iv.37. *oft adulter.* Another well known *crux.* The Second Quarto (again the only authority) reads *of a doubt* and has been variously emended. The reading here accepted is that of S. A. Tannenbaum (*Shaksperian Scraps*, 1933, p. 115). 'Adulter' for adulterate is a well established form, though not known to be used by Shakespeare elsewhere. If his manuscript abbreviated the last syllable in the common way (*oft adoult'*), the Quarto misprint is very easily explained.

I.iv.49. *inurn'd.* Put in an urn such as the Romans used for the ashes of their dead. There is a sharp inconsistency between this image and the previous one of bones bursting their cerements, but Shakespeare has the same confusion in *Henry V*, I.ii.228 f.:

> lay these bones in an unworthy urn,
> Tombless, with no remembrance over them.

(Both the Quartos read 'interr'd.')

I.iv.83. *Nemean lion's.* One of the powerful monsters slain by Hercules.

Prince of Denmark

I.v.21. *blazon.* Literally, to portray armorial bearings in their proper colors.

I.v.32. *the fat weed . . . Lethe wharf.* No particular weed, but an image of the absolute in vegetable nonchalance and inactivity. The Quarto reading, *rootes,* in line 33 is better than the Folio *rots.*

I.v.33. *Lethe.* A river (sometimes called a lake) of the Greek underworld, whose waters gave forgetfulness of the past to those who drank of them.

I.v.67. *gates and alleys.* Shakespeare here implies as much as was then known touching the circulation of the blood (Hudson).

I.v.80. *O horrible, etc.* The early texts print this line as part of the Ghost's speech, but the tradition of the stage is probably correct in assigning it to Hamlet. It was so spoken by, among others, Garrick, Kemble, and Irving. Betterton probably omitted it, for it is marked for omission in the Quarto of 1676.

I.v.136. *Saint Patrick.* He was the keeper of purgatory; the patron saint of all blunders and confusion (Moberly); he banished serpents from Ireland, hence he was the proper saint to take cognizance of the report that a serpent stung Hamlet's father (Dowden). If Hamlet's oath requires any explanation, the first surmise appears the more probable.

I.v.138. *honest ghost.* I.e., an actual ghost, and not the devil or an evil spirit in disguise. Note Hamlet's doubt upon this point later.

I.v.154. *sword.* It was customary to swear upon the sword, because the hilt made the form of the cross. Such an oath was binding both in military honor and in religion.

I.v.166. *your.* Does not mean Horatio's philosophy, but refers to philosophy in general. The Folio reads 'our.'

I.v.173. *With arms encumber'd thus, or this head-shake.* Mimicry goes with this, as Hamlet first folds his arms smugly and then nods his head.

II.i.40. *As 'twere a thing a little soil'd i' th' working.* As if Laertes were a gay new garment slightly smudged by the tailor's hands.

II.i.119. *More grief to hide than hate to utter love.* Polonius' syntax is more than usually overstrained as he attempts the oracular riming couplet. His meaning is: This love of Hamlet's must be made known, because if we kept it secret, more trouble might arise from its concealment than can displeasure from its revealing.

II.ii.11. *being of so young days brought up with him.* Rosencrantz and Guildenstern are noblemen who had been selected (as Kittredge remarks) to be Hamlet's schoolmates and playfellows when they were all children. Nothing indicates that they have been at the university. They appear to have been summoned to court from their country estates, quite in Queen Elizabeth's manner, and they arrive in some apprehension.

II.ii.44,45. *I hold my duty as I hold my soul, etc.* I think my duty, to both God and King, as important as my soul.

II.ii.61. *Upon our first.* Perhaps on hearing the first of the 'delated articles' mentioned in I.ii.38.

II.ii.73. *Gives him three thousand crowns in annual fee.* This line as here printed from the Folio has a Shakespearean rhythm that is destroyed in the Quarto version, 'Gives him threescore thousand crowns,' etc. Probably the Quarto printer felt, as modern editors have, that 3,000 crowns was not enough to wage a war; but an annual pension of that amount was a handsome encouragement (about equal to the thousand pounds Queen Elizabeth allowed her impoverished premier earl, the Earl of Oxford), and there is no reason to suppose that Norway means to subsidize the expedition. In any case, 60,000 crowns *in annual fee* (yearly income) would be fantastic.

II.ii.74. *his commission to employ those soldiers.* Something like the 'letters of marque' which make the difference between a privateer and a pirate.

II.ii.79. *regards . . . allowance. I.e.,* terms securing the safety of the country and regulating the passage of troops through it (Clarendon).

II.ii.112. *these, &.* That is, 'Deliver these lines.' The passage imitates the superscription of an Elizabethan letter.

II.ii.174. *fishmonger.* The word is probably used here in some cant coarse sense.

II.ii.182. *god kissing.* Bishop Warburton (1698–1779) suggested this emendation for 'good kissing' in the early editions. The sun's rays were supposed to engender maggots in dead flesh. Compare the reference to 'Titan' the sun god in *1 Henry IV,* II.iv.136 ff.

II.ii.194. *Between who?* Hamlet deliberately misunderstands 'matter' to mean a cause of dispute.

II.ii.199. *amber . . . gum.* In reference to the exudings from the weak eyes of old men.

II.ii.229–230. *on . . . button.* That is, we have not reached the summit of good fortune.

II.ii.237. *strumpet.* Because of Fortune's fickleness.

II.ii.265. *beggars bodies. I.e.,* if ambition is but a shadow, then

monarchs and heroes, who have attained ambition, are in possession only of a shadow; whereas beggars, who have not attained
ambition, at least possess something material—*i.e.*, their bodies.
But every beggar may long for ambition—a shadow—and hence
the monarchs and heroes who are in possession of their ambi-
tions, are but the beggars' shadows—*i.e.*, have this shadow for
which the beggar longs in vain.

II.ii.277. *too dear a halfpenny.* A little too dear. Even my poor
thanks are worth more than the visitation for which I am
thanking you, for that is not a genuine kindness.

II.ii.312. *quintessence.* A term in alchemy. The fifth essence of
ancient and mediæval philosophy, supposed to be the substance
of which the heavenly bodies were composed, and to be
actually latent in all things: hence, pure essence or extract,
essential part of a thing (O. E. D.)

II.ii.326. *humorous man.* It would appear that there is particular
reference here to the audience's interruption of Macilente's part
in Jonson's *Every Man out of his Humour* when Shakespeare's
company first produced that play in 1599. The following passage on the clown, like Hamlet's rebuke in III.ii.39 ff., is doubtless pointed at Will Kempe, the popular comic actor and
dancer, who left the company in displeasure shortly before
Shakespeare's *Hamlet* was produced.

II.ii.328. *tickle o' the sere.* Literally, the 'sere' is the catch of a
gunlock that holds the hammer. Hence a trigger that goes off
at a light touch. The Folio spells: 'tickled a' th' sere'.

II.ii.336. *the late innovation.* The new popularity of the companies of child-actors, the Children of the Queen's Chapel and
Children of Paul's, both of which re-opened their theatres about
1600.

II.ii.338. *the city.* London is meant. What follows is highly topi-
cal and refers to conditions during the 'War of the Theatres' of
1600 and 1601.

II.ii.342. *aery of children.* The Children of the Queen's Chapel
are particularly meant.

II.ii.345. *common stages.* The public theatres, such as the Globe,
which were less aristocratic than the private houses occupied by
the children.

II.ii.346. *afraid of goose-quills.* The goose-quills are the pens of
satirical dramatists, especially Ben Jonson. His *Poetaster,* acted
by the Chapel Children in 1601, is full of ridicule of the adult
players, with whom he had temporarily quarrelled.

II.ii.364. *Hercules and his load.* The reference may be to the sign of the Globe Theatre which represented Hercules carrying the globe. The sign itself was an allusion to the story of Hercules relieving Atlas.

II.ii.382. *I know a hawk from a handsaw.* I know one thing from another. An old proverb. (A 'handsaw' is a hernshaw or heron.)

II.ii.394. *Roscius.* A famous Roman actor of Cicero's time, whose intellectual capacities lifted him above the stigma usually attached to his profession.

II.ii.402. *scene individable.* A play which follows the classical rules relating to the three unities of time, place, and action.

II.ii.402–403. *poem unlimited.* A play which disregarded the unities. *Seneca.* A Roman writer of rhetorical tragedies (died 65 A.D.) whose plays were during the Renaissance considered models of classic technique. *Plautus.* A Roman comic dramatist of the third century B.C. who ranked with Terence as the model for comedy. Imitated by Shakespeare in *The Comedy of Errors.*

II.ii.404. *law of writ and the liberty.* Polonius may be only repeating the distinction between 'scene individable' and 'poem unlimited' above. It is possible that *law of writ* refers to rehearsed performances following the written text, and *liberty* to plays in which the dialogue was extemporized by the actors, as in the Italian *commedia dell' arte.*

II.ii.431. *Cracked . . . ring.* Having the circle broken that surrounds the sovereign's head on a coin. Here used quibblingly for a voice that has changed and hence is 'cracked' in its 'ring' or purity of tone. It is, of course, a boy actor of women's parts that Hamlet is addressing.

II.ii.440. *Caviary . . . general.* I.e., a delicacy (caviar) for which the general public had no relish.

II.ii.444. *no sallets . . . savory.* No ribaldry to spice the lines.

II.ii.448. *handsome.* I.e., its beauty was not that of elaborate diction or polish, but that of structure and proportion.

II.ii.449. *Æneas' tale to Dido.* The passage inserted here should be compared with Marlowe's *Dido, Queen of Carthage* (1594), II.i.213 ff. It is a matter of critical dispute whether Shakespeare intended this passage as burlesque or whether he selected deliberately the earlier turgid romantic style to contrast with his more realistic dramatic method in this scene. The Marlowe play had been acted by the 'little eyases' (Children of the Chapel) and was probably still in their repertoire in 1601.

II.ii.453. *Hyrcanian beast.* The tiger. So described by Virgil. Cf. *Æneid,* IV. 367.

II.ii.457. *ominous horse.* The wooden horse in which the Greeks lay hidden until the Trojans dragged it within the walls.

II.ii.531. *God's bodkin.* A corruption of an oath 'by God's body.'

II.ii.540. *the Murther of Gonzago.* No such play is recorded, but S. A. Tannenbaum has dealt with two historical murders in the Gonzaga family (*Shakspere Assoc. Bull.,* xvi, 1941, 169–74).

II.ii.543. *some dozen or sixteen lines.* A colloquial way of indicating an uncertain small number, as we say 'ten or twelve' (Hamlet has not yet written the speech). So Baxter says: 'When he had been a preacher about twelve or sixteen years.'

II.ii.564. *cue.* A technical stage term for the last words of an actor's line to which another actor replied.

II.ii.572. *John-a-dreams.* Armin's *Nest of Ninnies* (1608) contains the following definition: 'His name is John, indeed, says the cynic; but neither John-a-nods, nor John-a-dreams, yet either as you take it, for he is simply simple without tricks.'

II.ii.574. *property.* His crown, his wife, everything, in short, which he might be said to be possessed of, except his life (Furness).

II.ii.581. *pigeon-liver'd.* It was believed that pigeons were gentle because they had no gall.

II.ii.588. *murthered.* Pronounce in three syllables. Only the bad First Quarto has 'father', which is not needed.

III.i.13. *Niggard of question, etc.* This report differs wholly from the facts. Rosencrantz and Guildenstern are not malign, but they have to save their faces.

III.i.56. *To be, or not to be.* To live or die. This is the lowest point that Hamlet's melancholy reaches. In the suspense with which he awaits the outcome of his test, he loses the glad assurance with which he closed Act II (the day before), and allows himself to wonder how any sensitive person can consent to endure the humiliations of life. He argues, however, in general terms, not in terms of his own situation.

III.i.59. *take . . . troubles.* Many commentators have felt that this line contains a badly mixed metaphor and consequently have suggested various unnecessary emendations. The phrase 'sea of troubles,' in the sense of a 'mass of troubles,' however, occurs elsewhere in Elizabethan literature. Cf. Greene's *Mamil-*

lia, ed. Grosart, vol. II., p. 18; "hauing himself escaped the sea, of trouble and care," and Dekker's *The Wonder of a Kingdome*, ed. 1873, vol. IV., p. 230:

> I never heard mongst all your Romane spirits,
> That any held so bravely up his head,
> In such a sea of troubles (that come rouling
> One on anothers necke) as Lotti doth.

III.i.69. *makes calamity of so long life.* Makes affliction (*i.e.*, the afflicted person) live so long.

III.i.70—74. *For who would bear, etc.* The miseries specified are more those of man in general than of the Prince of Denmark. (In line 72 the Quarto reads *despiz'd*.)

III.i.76. *a bare bodkin.* This may mean 'a mere pin' or 'an unsheathed dagger.' The former is more forceful.

III.i.80. *No traveller returns.* The ghost is ignored. In this soliloquy Hamlet's mind is curiously stripped of the religious ideas and implications which usually mark it.

III.i.118. *virtue cannot so inoculate our old stock.* A figure from the grafting of apples, with a hint at Eve's apple and original sin. Acquired virtue may be grafted on the old sinful tree ('stock'), but the fruit will still taste of man's fall.

III.i.121. *Get thee to a nunnery.* For which Ophelia's devotional apparatus and attitude qualify her. The sense of futility expressed in the preceding soliloquy here turns to misanthropy.

III.i.131. *Where's your father?* Hamlet here sees Polonius, and in line 151 ('all but one') he sees the king. There is no reason to believe that he is aware of their presence earlier.

III.i.148. *nickname. I.e.*, by painting your face and by your fashionable affectations you turn human beings (God's creatures) into figures that bear the same resemblance to reality that a nickname does to a Christian name. Or possibly this is an allusion to the Elizabethan court fashion of giving animal names to the various courtiers.

III.ii.11. *groundlings.* The inferior portion of the audience who paid a penny for standing room in the yard or pit. *Hamlet* was written for a courtly, not a popular, audience, and perhaps in deliberate effort to establish the prestige which the 'little eyases' were endangering.

III.ii.12. *inexplicable dumb-shows.* Pantomimes illustrating the subsequent action of the play, such as began each act of *Gorboduc* and other early tragedies.

III.ii.14. *Termagant.* A noisy character representing a supposed god of the Saracens in some of the mystery plays.

III.ii.14. *out-herods Herod. I.e.,* outdoes even the extravagant acting of Herod, the most violent and declamatory figure in the mystery plays. Cf. the stage direction in the Coventry play of the *Magi and Herod,* 'Here Herod rages in the pageant, and in the street also.'

III.ii.41. *there be of them, etc.* Examples of gags and stage business introduced by clowns are found in a contemporary anonymous play, *The Pilgrimage to Parnassus,* Act V, ll. 680 ff.:
'if thou canst but draw thy mouth awry, lay thy leg over thy staff, saw a piece of cheese asunder with thy dagger, lap up drink on the earth, I warrant thee they'll laugh mightily.'

III.ii.69. *co-mingled.* The Folio reading. Q2 has *comedled* (commeddled), which would mean the same thing.

III.ii.70. *a pipe for fortune's finger, etc.* This image of the 'recorder' is elaborately developed later in the scene, ll. 346 ff.

III.ii.81. *in one speech.* While one speech of the play is being spoken. Claudius is not expected to make a speech (cf. lines 84–89 below), but to betray his guilt by the look on his face.

III.ii.84. *Vulcan.* He was the armorer of the gods.

III.ii.90. *be idle.* In Hall's Chronicle, the phrase 'idle and weak in his wit' occurs (*O.E.D.*).

III.ii.93. *chameleon's dish.* It was believed that chameleons fed on air. (Hamlet takes the King's question in the sense, 'How are you being fed?')

III.ii.103. *Julius Cæsar.* The universities gave many representations within their walls of plays in Latin and occasionally English. A Latin play on Cæsar's death by Richard Edes was acted at Christ Church, Oxford, in 1582. See also the title-page of the 1603 Quarto of Hamlet.

III.ii.104. *Capitol.* The murder of Cæsar actually took place in the Theatre of Pompey, which stood in the Campus Martius. Shakespeare transfers the scene to the Capitol both in *Julius Cæsar* and in *Antony and Cleopatra.*

III.ii.116. *country.* For the hidden pun see Farmer & Henley, *Slang and its Analogues,* ii. p. 230.

III.ii.129. *twice two months.* This implies that about two months have passed since the opening of the play (cf. I.ii.138). Most of this time elapsed in the interval between Act I and Act II.

III.ii.131. *I'll have a suit of sables.* Hamlet's persiflage is ambiguous. Sable fur was brown and connoted not mourning but wealth and elegance, but 'sable' as an adjective in heraldry meant black. The sense of the double talk is perhaps (1) Let the devil now wear my black mourning, for I'll be dressed like a normal prince; (2) Let the devil wear black, for I shall be dressed just like him.

III.ii.135. *hobby-horse.* In the morris dance, a figure of a horse made of light material and fastened around the waist of a performer, who went through various antics. The quotation here may be from a ballad perhaps satirizing Puritan opposition to May-games.

III.ii.139. *miching Malicho.* The Quarto has *munching Mallico.* The second word is usually taken to be Spanish 'malhecho,' which does mean 'mischief' or 'misdeed.' Eric Partridge ('Some Romany Words,' London *Times Literary Supplement*, Dec. 26, 1936) argues for a Gypsy origin.

III.ii.158. *Tellus'.* The goddess of the earth, who received and nourished the sown seed. *Orbed ground* is the round earth.

III.ii.220. *Sport and repose.* Here the objects of the verb.

III.ii.241. *Tropically.* By means of a trope or figure of speech; but the bad First Quarto prints 'Trapically,' which (with reference to the Mousetrap) is what Hamlet secretly means.

III.ii.243. *duke's name.* In the First Quarto the leading characters are called Duke and Duchess. In the Second Quarto and the Folio, except for this line, they are always King and Queen.

III.ii.250. *interpret.* At puppet shows or 'motions' the dialogue was spoken by a person concealed behind the stage. This was called 'interpreting.' The classic example is the 'motion' of Hero and Leander presented by Lanthorn Leatherhead in Jonson's *Bartholomew Fair* (1614), V.iv.

III.ii.256. *So you must take your husbands.* That is, 'for better, for worse.' The good texts here have 'mistake' for *must take,* found only in the bad First Quarto.

III.ii.258. *the croaking . . . revenge.* Parody of a non-Shakespearean play of 1594, *The True Tragedy of Richard the Third* (Malone *Society* reprint, ll. 1892f.)

> The screeking raven sits croking for revenge,
> Whole herds of beasts come bellowing for revenge,

III.ii.262. *Hecate.* Diana, in her aspect as infernal goddess, was regarded as the queen of witches. Pronounce 'Hecat's'.

III.ii.275. *deer go weep.* It was a popular belief that the deer, when badly wounded, retires from the herd and goes apart to weep and die. See *As You Like It*, II.i.33–43.

III.ii.281. *Provincial roses.* So called from Provins, a town forty miles from Paris.

III.ii.282. *cry.* Literally, a pack of hounds—here, troop or company.

III.ii.283. *share.* Theatrical companies were organized on a profit-sharing basis. The controlling members were called 'sharers' and the original 'shares' could be subdivided.

III.ii.285. *Damon.* An allusion to the classical story of the friendship of Damon and Pythias (or Phintias), dramatized by Richard Edwards in a play printed in 1571.

III.ii.288. *pajock.* 'A king of shreds and patches,' as Hamlet calls him a little later (iv.103). The word has nothing to do with peacock, but is the same that Spenser uses, in the form 'patchock' or 'patchcock' to describe the degenerate English in Ireland. The realm, Hamlet says, has been 'dismantled' of his father (as if gorgeous raiment had been removed), and now they have in his place a ragamuffin. (The *O.E.D.* has conjecturally explained this, but editors have ignored the explanation.)

III.ii.304. *distempered.* This word was used both of mental and of bodily disorder. Hamlet pretends to understand it in the latter sense.

III.ii.306. *choler.* The other meaning of 'choler' is bilious disorder, and so again Hamlet pretends to misunderstand it.

III.ii.309. *purgation.* Another word of double meaning: (1) clearing from the accusation or suspicion of guilt; (2) purging in the medical sense.

III.ii.318. *this courtesy is not of the right breed.* Guildenstern does not think Hamlet to be mad and he knows that he is being laughed at. Here, with real dignity, he withdraws from the conversation and leaves Rosencrantz to take it up.

III.ii.339. *pickers and stealers.* An allusion to the phrase in the Catechism, 'To keep my hands from picking and stealing.'

III.ii.346. *'While . . . grows.'* A proverb of frequent occurrence. Cf. Heywood's *Proverbs* "while the grass groweth the horse sterveth," and Whetstone's *Promos and Cassandra* (1578), "Whylst grass doth growe, oft sterves the seely steede."

III.ii.349. *recover the wind of.* A hunting term, meaning to frighten the game by approaching in the direction of the wind.

III.ii.359. *I know no touch of it.* Guildenstern is emphatic. Wind instruments were not in favor with fine gentlemen. They distorted the mouth.

III.ii.374. *fret.* Frets are stops of instruments of the lute or guitar kind. Hamlet also uses it quibblingly to mean 'annoy.'

III.ii.387. *the top of my bent.* An expression derived from archery; the bow has its 'bent' when it is drawn as far as it can be. Compare II.ii.30.

III.ii.397. *Nero.* He murdered his mother, Agrippina.

III.iii.7. *braves.* The Quarto reading is 'browes,' for which the Folio substitutes (apparently in desperation) 'Lunacies.' The word here accepted is an ancient anonymous conjecture, independently revived in *Yale Review* (March, 1935, p. 620) and in the Parrott-Craig ed. (1938).

III.iii.17–22. *It is a massy wheel, etc.* This passage is an interesting development of the earlier image of Fortune's wheel (II.ii.497–499).

III.iii.30. *as you said.* Polonius knows that the proposal came from himself. Compare III.i.185–189.

III.iii.37. *primal.* The curse of Cain. Cf. Genesis 4. 11: 'And now art thou cursed from the earth, which hath opened her mouth to receive thy brother's blood from thy hand.'

III.iii.61. *lies.* Is sustainable as an action at law.

III.iii.73. *pat.* This famous word is not in the Quarto text, which has 'but' instead.

III.iii.79. *hire and salary.* The Folio reading. Q2 has 'base and silly.'

III.iv.99. *vice.* The Vice was a stock character in the Moralities and Interludes. Although personifying the weaker side of human nature, he was represented as a buffoon and supplied much of the comic element in these plays.

III.iv.103. *A king of shreds and patches.* A mock king dressed in oddments of costume, such as one might see in a peasant folk-play. This line points the contrast with the ghost, who here enters in peaceful dress—'in his nightgown,' or robe of velvet and fur, according to Q1.

III.iv.169. *tame.* A word has dropped out of the Quarto text.

III.iv.192–196. *The famous ape.* The moral of this unidentified parable is that the Queen will destroy herself, if she allows Hamlet's secrets (the birds) to get abroad or attempts to introduce herself into his business.

III.iv.211. *packing.* A pun: (1) preparing for my journey; (2) plotting, using my wits (Dover Wilson).

III.v.4. The Folio text indicates that the King enters alone to the Queen after Hamlet has dragged out Polonius' body (without any change of scene).

III.v.7. *Mad as the sea and wind, etc.* The queen's report attempts to free Hamlet of responsibility for Polonius' death. She does not really think him mad, but avoids doing what Hamlet has instructed her not to do. See III.iv.180–188.

III.v.40. *So, haply, slander.* Added by Theobald and Capell.

III.vi.17. *like an ape an apple.* A composite reading suggested by Farmer. The Second Quarto has 'like an apple,' the Folio 'like an Ape,' the bad First Quarto 'as an Ape doth nuttes.'

III.vi.27. *The . . . body.* A passage about which there have been many conjectures. If Hamlet is not designedly talking mere nonsense, a possible interpretation is: "The King is still alive (*i.e.,* with *his* body), but he is not with the dead body (*i.e.,* of Polonius)."

III.vi.28,30. *a thing . . . of nothing.* Quoting the Prayer Book version of Psalm 144. 4, 'Man is like a thing of nought.'

III.vi.30. *Hide fox, and all after.* Added in the Folio, probably to motivate Hamlet's sudden rush from the stage. Compare that of King Lear, *Lear,* IV.vi.207.

III.vii.21. *convocation.* Perhaps an allusion to the famous Diet or convocation of the dignitaries of the German Empire held at Worms in 1521. It was before this Diet that Martin Luther was summoned to appear.

IV.i.s.d. Here the Folio omits the Gentleman, no doubt, as Collier suggested, to avoid the employment of another actor. A time interval of about a month occurs at this point, and this is the logical place to begin Act IV. Most editors continue the eighteenth century act division, which begins Act IV with III.v, because it has become conventional. (This was apparently Betterton's division, being indicated in the text of 1676.)

IV.i.20.,S.d. The direction in the First Quarto of 1603 is, 'Enter Ofelia playing on a lute, and her haire downe, singing.' This is the basis for the traditional stage-business.

IV.i.25. *cockle hat.* The cockle hat, staff, and sandals were the guise of a pilgrim and often the disguise of a lover. Cf. Romeo's costume at the ball in *Romeo and Juliet.* The hat was so called from the custom of putting cockle-shells upon pilgrims' hats. The shell was used to denote that the pilgrim had been to the shrine of St. James of Compostella in Spain.

IV.i.39. *did—not—go.* The word *not* breaks the rhythm of the

song and is perhaps Ophelia's comment on the lack of cere-
monious burial for Polonius.

IV.i.42. *owl . . . daughter.* There is an old mediæval legend
that a baker's daughter was turned into an owl for refusing
bread to our Lord (Douce).

IV.i.97. *Switzers.* The Pope and the kings of France employed
Swiss mercenaries as guards. The term 'Switzer' gradually became almost synonymous with 'guard.'

IV.i.142. *swoopstake.* A gambling term used when the winner
clears the board of all the stakes.

IV.i.146. *life-rendering pelican.* It was a common belief that the
pelican fed its young with its own blood. It was thus an emblem of family devotion.

IV.i.161–163. *Nature is fine in love, etc.* When we love, nature
refines or subtilizes us so that some precious part of ourselves
goes like an 'instance' (memento or farewell gift) after what
we love. Thus Ophelia's wits have followed Polonius in death.

IV.i.165. *Hey non nonny.* Such meaningless refrains are common
in old songs. Cf. 170, 'a-down.'

IV.i.172. *wheel.* Although this word is usually rendered 'burden,'
'refrain,' it is possible that Ophelia is referring to singing at
the spinning wheel.

IV.i.172. *false steward.* This ballad or story is unknown.

IV.i.175. *rosemary.* Flower symbolism was an elaborate system in
mediæval and Elizabethan England. Cf. *The Handfull of
Pleasant Delights* (1584):

> Rosemarie is for remembrance,
> betweene vs daie and night:
> Wishing that I might alwaies haue
> you present in my sight.

Rosemary was often strewn on biers. Cf. *Romeo and Juliet,*
IV.v.79; *Winter's Tale,* IV.iii.74.

IV.i.176. *pansies.* French, *pensées;* a country emblem of love and
courtship.

IV.i.182. *herb of grace.* Simply another popular name for rue.
Cf. *Richard II,* III.iv.105 f.:

> I'll set a bank of rue, sour herb of grace;
> Rue, even for ruth, here shortly shall be seen.

IV.i.183. *difference.* An heraldic bearing, distinguishing the arms
of one branch of the same family from another. Ophelia im-

plies that for the Queen rue signifies the remembrance of things to be repented, for herself regret.

IV.i.186. *For . . . joy.* The music for this song is contained in Anthony Holborne's *Citharn Schoole* (1597) and other collections. The words have not been found.

IV.iii.8. *As by your safety, greatness, wisdom, all things.* The Quarto adds *els* (else) at the end of the line, a weak superfluity probably due to scribe or compositor. The Folio keeps *else,* but omits *greatness* to make the line scan.

IV.iii.20. *Work.* The Second Quarto reading, certainly correct. The Folio has 'Would,' probably the printer's accidental anticipation of that word in line 23. Shakespeare would not willingly, and no editor should, put 'Would . . . wood' in the same line.

IV.iii.20. *spring.* There are several springs in England whose water is so heavily charged with lime that they will petrify with a deposit of lime any object placed in them. There is one at King's Newnham in Warwickshire and another at Knaresborough in Yorkshire.

IV.iii.23. *reverted.* I.e., the 'loud wind' of popular affection for Hamlet would have caused Claudius' shafts to recoil upon himself.

IV.iii.27. *praises . . . again.* I.e., if praises may return to what is now no more, *viz.,* Ophelia's former charms.

IV.iii.28. *challenger-on-mount.* I.e., her worth challenged all the age to deny her perfection.

IV.iii.40. *Claudio.* A character who does not appear in the play. Cf. IV.ii.29.

IV.iii.75. *siege.* Literally 'seat,' thence 'rank,' because people sat at table in order of precedence.

IV.iii.86. *incorps'd and demi-natur'd.* I.e., like a Centaur, half horse, half man. Literally, of one body with and half partaking of the nature of his horse.

IV.iii.88. *in . . . tricks.* I.e., I cannot describe so many proofs of dexterity as he performed.

IV.iii.91. *Lamound.* So the Folio calls him; the Quarto 'Lamord.'

IV.iii.95. *masterly report.* A report describing Laertes as a master of fence.

IV.iii.104. *to play with you.* That he might fence with you. Not understanding, the Folio adopts the easier reading, 'to play with him.'

IV.iii.111. *passages of proof.* Instances from practical experience of the world.

IV.iii.116. *plurisy*. Often used where today one would say 'plethora' (because of a false association with Latin *plus*).

IV.iii.121. *spendthrift's sigh*. A satisfactory paraphrase has not been suggested. The general meaning is probably that the recognition of a 'should' when it is too late is like a wasteful or supererogatory sigh of the spendthrift who recalls his lost opportunities. The sighs are also spendthrifts on the old notion that each one drained blood from the heart (cf. *M.N.D.*, III.ii.97).

IV.iii.140. *mountebank*. These men were quack-doctors who journeyed from town to town selling miraculous remedies and forbidden poisons. The classical account of their procedure is given in Ben Jonson's play, *Volpone*, Act II, sc. ii.

IV.iii.144. *moon*. It was believed that to gather herbs by moonlight added to their medicinal value. It is possible, however, that here the meaning is simply 'on earth.'

IV.iii.150. *that our drift look through our bad performance*. If our design should become visible by the bad execution of the plot. The image is apparently of the moon looking through thin clouds.

IV.iii.152. *a back or second*. Support or auxiliary. The king and Laertes are bungling plotters, unused and by temperament unsuited to the niceties of crime.

IV.iii.169. *crowflowers*. It is probable that Shakespeare is still carrying on his flower symbolism in the garlands worn by Ophelia. Thus the crowflower was also called 'the fair maid of France'; long purples were said to represent the cold hand of death; nettles meant 'stung to the quick'; and the daisy sometimes imported 'pure virginity' or 'spring of life' (Parkinson).

IV.iii.189. *woman*. I.e., when these tears are shed the woman in me, what I have inherited from my mother, will have come out.

V.i.S.d. *Clowns*. The term applies both to peasants and to actors of low comedy rôles. It seems likely that this scene was inspired by a local incident which occurred when Shakespeare was in his sixteenth year. Katharine Hamlet (*sic*), spinster, was drowned in the River Avon, Dec. 17, 1579, and the coroner's jury sat on her for eight weeks, at last finding it Christian burial. (See E. I. Fripp, *Shakespeare Studies*, 1930, pp. 128–136; and for text of the inquest *Minutes & Accounts of the Corporation of Stratford-upon-Avon*, 1926, vol. iii. p. 50.)

V.i.9. *se offendendo*. The clown's mistake for *se defendendo*, which would itself be a mistake, since this was the verdict in the case of justifiable homicide, not, of course, suicide.

V.i.34. *bore arms.* A quibble on bearing a coat of arms and the literal meaning.

V.i.40. *confess thyself.* Half of an old proverb. The rest was 'and be hanged.' Or possibly 'confess thyself a fool.'

V.i.53. *unyoke.* Literally, 'you may then free your cattle from the yoke'; hence, 'call it a day's work.'

V.i.61. *Yaughan.* Phonetic Danish for 'John' (Johan). The name is in the Folio text, but not in the Quarto, which reads simply, 'Go, get thee *in*,' etc. It may be a local joke, added by the actors. Jonson's *Alchemist*, acted by Shakespeare's company at the Blackfriars theatre in 1610, refers to 'an ale-house darker than deaf John's' (I.i.85), as if the latter were well and unfavorably known. If Yaughan and deaf John kept the same establishment, this reference cannot be earlier than 1609, when Shakespeare's company began using the Blackfriars.

V.i.63. *In . . . love.* This song, by Lord Vaux, is found in Tottel's *Miscellany* (1557) under the title *The aged louer renounceth loue*, although the Clown sings a confused and blundering version of it.

V.i.69. *property of easiness.* I.e., custom has made it natural to him to take his task easily.

V.i.79. Legend asserted that Cain slew Abel with the jaw-bone of an ass.

V.i.81. *o'erreaches.* A quibble on two meanings: (1) 'paws over,' (2) 'outwits.' This is the Quarto reading; the Folio has 'o'eroffices.'

V.i.87. *went to beg it.* This is the reading of the Second Quarto, justified by O.E.D. (*Go* 34,b). The Folio changes 'went' to 'meant,' which looks like a printer's emendation.

V.i.94. *loggats.* A game in which thick sticks are thrown to lie as near as possible to a stake fixed in the ground or to a block of wood on a floor.

V.i.102. *tenures.* The act, right, or manner of holding, as real estate, property of a superior; manner in, or period for, which anything is had and enjoyed. As the present passage shows, Shakespeare's knowledge of legal terminology was broad, but it was not extraordinary for his time or minutely professional. (See P. S. Clarkson and C. T. Warren, *The Law of Property in Shakespeare and the Elizabethan Drama*, 1942.)

V.i.105. *action of battery.* Right to sue for an unlawful attack by beating and wounding.

V.i.107. *statutes.* Particular modes of recognizance or acknowledgment for securing debts, which thereby became a charge upon the party's land (Ritson).

V.i.107. *recognizances.* Bonds or obligations of record testifying the recognizor to owe to the recognizee a certain sum of money.

V.i.108. *vouchers.* Persons who are called upon to warrant a tenant's title.

V.i.108. *fines, recoveries.* Processes by which entailed estates were commonly transferred from one party to another.

V.i.112. *the length . . . indentures.* That is, a couple of his legal papers will cover all the ground he has left; *i.e.,* his grave.

V.i.113. *conveyances.* Documents by which transference of property is effected.

V.i.119. *assurance.* Also used with quibble on its legal meaning 'evidence of the conveyance or settlement of property.'

V.i.142. *by the card.* The card on which the thirty-two points of the mariner's compass are marked.

V.i.144. *this three years . . . the age is grown so picked.* There is a temptation to associate this with the era of social sophistication which became strikingly articulate in Jonson's *Every Man in his Humor* (1598). Compare the talk of contemporary drama in II.ii.340 ff.

V.i.178. *three-and-twenty years.* We have here further testimony in support of the Clown's earlier statement (lines 151, 165 f.) that Hamlet was about thirty years old. This is evidently purposed and is not contradicted by anything else in the play. Shakespeare may, however, have begun with the idea of a younger prince and have been brought to emphasize his maturity at the end, both by the way the character developed and by the consideration that Richard Burbage (born about 1567) was outgrowing youthful parts.

V.i.185. *Sir Yorick's.* The text follows the Quarto. Yorick was not a knight, but, from the Clown at least, may well rate the honorific awarded to country parsons and bachelors of arts. The name might be meant for George (Georg) as pronounced in Danish. Relations between London and Denmark were close in Queen Elizabeth's reign, and grew closer when James I, with his Danish queen, came to the throne in 1603.

V.i.223. *but soft awhile!* This, the reading of the Second Quarto, is probably what Shakespeare first wrote. The Folio version, 'but soft, aside,' works the necessary business of stepping aside into the line, but that action is covered by line 228.

V.i.234. *And but that great command o'ersways the order.* Except that sovereign power (the king's command) prevails over the rules of the religious order to which the priest belongs. (He corroborates the suspicion of the Clowns in lines 24—30.) Here as elsewhere in the play, the tone is Catholic. In Q 2 the priest's two speeches are assigned to 'Doct.,' whatever that may mean.

V.i.235. *should . . . been lodg'd.* This old-fashioned construction, perfectly normal in earlier English, was modernized in the Folio 'should . . . have lodg'd.'

V.i.238. *crants.* German *Kranz* (singular, not plural). Garlands appear to have been borne before the bodies of unmarried women to the grave, and were hung up in church.

V.i.259. *Pelion.* Pelion, Olympus, and Ossa (l. 289) are three mountains in the north of Thessaly. The Titans, warring with the gods, are said to have attempted to pile Ossa on Pelion in an effort to scale Olympus.

V.i.264. *Hamlet the Dane.* Thus naming himself, he asserts his royal rank and further infuriates Laertes. The stage direction accompanying this line is found only in the bad First Quarto.

V.i.293. *golden couplets.* The dove lays but two eggs and the young, when first disclosed, are covered with a yellow down. Cf. III.i.168 f.

V.ii.13. *sea-gown.* 'A coarse, high-collared and short-sleeved gown, reaching down to the mid leg, and used most by seamen and sailors' (Onions).

V.ii.22. *bugs . . . life.* I.e., with such enumeration of bugbears and imaginary terrors if Hamlet were allowed to live.

V.ii.30. *prologue . . . play.* I.e., before I had formed any real plan, my brains had begun their work.

V.ii.42. *comma.* A symbol of relation between two parts of the same whole.

V.ii.43. *'As'es.* A quibble on 'as,' the conditional particle, and 'ass,' the beast of burden.

V.ii.61. *pass and fell-incensed points.* Hendiadys: the angrily thrusting sword points.

V.ii.65. *election.* The Danish throne was elective.

V.ii.84. *water-fly.* Used for a vain or idly busy person, but probably also with reference to the gaudy attire of the foolish courtier.

V.ii.89. *mess.* 'One of the groups of persons, normally four, into which the company at a banquet was divided' (Onions).

V.ii.106. *remember.* The phrase 'remember thy courtesy' (*i.e.,* remember that you are bareheaded) was a conventional one for 'be covered.' Cf. *Love's Labour's Lost,* V.i.106.

V.ii.107. *my ease.* This again was the conventional apologetic reply for declining the invitation of 'remember thy courtesy.'

V.ii.117. *yaw.* Nautical figure: to make way sideward, as from bad steering.

V.ii.127. *another tongue.* Any tongue but his own.

V.ii.157. *edified by the margent.* Equivalent to looking up a word in the glossary. It was customary to print explanatory matter in the margins of Elizabethan books.

V.ii.169. *twelve for nine.* The exact details of this wager are a matter of doubt.

V.ii.195. *fond and winnowed.* So the Folio, meaning perhaps 'foolish and trite (well sifted).' The Quarto reads *prophane and trennowed,* the latter word being an easy misreading of 'winnowed.' This portion of the play was largely unintelligible to the printers of both the early texts.

V.ii.248. *satisfied in nature.* Though his natural anger as a son is satisfied with Hamlet's explanation, yet his artificial honor as a courtier requires that the matter shall be adjudicated.

V.ii.259. *foil.* That which sets something off to advantage, with a quibble on the meaning 'fencing foil.'

V.ii.273. *quit.* I.e., requite Laertes' winning of the first two bouts by gaining the third.

V.ii.306.s.d. The usual method of representing upon the stage this exchange of rapiers is as follows: With a quick thrust Hamlet disarms Laertes. As the foil drops, Hamlet places his foot upon it, and, with a bow, offers Laertes his own in exchange. Courtesy compels Laertes to accept this, after which Hamlet stoops, picks up Laertes' foil from the ground, and resumes the bout. For a technical discussion see James L. Jackson, 'The Exchange of Weapons in *Hamlet*' (*Mod. Lang. Notes,* Jan., 1942).

V.ii.344. *Roman.* It was a Roman custom to follow masters in death. See *Julius Caesar,* V. iii; *A. & C.,* IV. xii.

V.ii.355. *This warlike volley.* This suggests that the 'shout' mentioned in the Folio s.d. at line 352 should be 'shot.'

V.ii.361. *solicited.* The sentence is left unfinished.

V.ii.367. *cries on havoc.* Originally, to give an army the order 'havoc!' as the signal for pillaging.

V.ii.401. *royal.* The word is very strongly stressed, almost drawn out to three syllables. The Folio weakens by changing it to 'royally.'

V.ii.403. *Speak.* A command: let music, *etc.*, speak.

APPENDIX A

Sources of the Play

THERE are two early references to the name 'Hamlet,' or 'Amleth,' one (spelled in Irish fashion 'Amhlaide') in *The Annals of Ireland by the Four Masters*,[1] under the year 917, and the other (spelled 'Amlothi') in Snorri's *Prose Edda*, about three centuries later.[2] The outline of the story of Hamlet, as we are familiar with it, is first found in the *Historia Danica* of Saxo Grammaticus, a Danish chronicler who lived at the end of the twelfth century.[3]

Saxo's version contains the following elements in common with Shakespeare's: the murder of Hamlet's father by the latter's ambitious brother; the mother's incestuous marriage with the murderer; the son's feigned madness, or "folly," for the purpose of carrying out his revenge; a foreshadowing of the character of Ophelia by the girl thrown in Hamlet's way that the true state of his mind may be discovered; a foreshadowing of the character of Polonius; the scene between mother and son;[4] the voyage to England with two companions, during which Hamlet alters the letter, and the companions are put to death in his stead; Hamlet's return to kill his uncle, a deed which he accomplishes. The ending differs.

[1] Cf. the Introduction to Gollancz's *Hamlet in Iceland*, p. li.

[2] For an attempt to reconstruct the primitive plot see the last chapter in *The Literary History of Hamlet. I. The Early Tradition*, by Kemp Malone (1923).

[3] For most of the materials here referred to see Sir Israel Gollancz, *The Sources of Hamlet*, 1926.

[4] Cf. *Hamlet*, III. iv.

François de Belleforest published about 1570 a free translation of Saxo's Hamlet story in French prose in the fifth book of his *Histoires Tragiques*. Although many editions of this appeared in France before 1600, there is no evidence of an English version before the publication by Thomas Pavier of the *Hystorie of Hamblet* in 1608. This English translation differs in a few particulars from Belleforest, and these differences seem to be due to the influence of Shakespeare's play. Thus, in Belleforest the counsellor who acts the spy during Amleth's (Hamlet's) interview with his mother, conceals himself under a bed-quilt, upon which Amleth leaps when entering the room and so discovers the eavesdropper. In the *Hystorie*, the counsellor hides behind the arras, as in the play. Again, Hamblet, at the moment of this discovery, calls out "A rat! A rat!," of which there is no trace in Belleforest.

There is another, and more direct, source for Shakespeare's play, *viz.*, an earlier play by another author on the same subject. The evidence for the existence of such a work is as follows: In 1589 was published Greene's *Menaphon* with a prefatory epistle by Thomas Nashe "to the Gentlemen Students of both Vniuersities." In this epistle, Nashe briefly reviews contemporary literature and refers to "whole Hamlets, I should say Handfuls, of tragical speeches," linking this remark with a reference to Seneca.

The next reference to an early play of Hamlet is from the *Diary* of Philip Henslowe,[1] the theatrical manager, for the year 1594.

"Ye 9 of June 1594. R[eceive]d. at hamlet, viijs". At

---

[1] The entry differs from those Henslowe made when the play mentioned was a new one.

this time the Lord Chamberlain's and the Lord Admiral's men were playing for Henslowe at the theatre at Newington Butts. The former company was the one to which Shakespeare belonged.

Lodge's *Wit's Misery, and the World's Madness,* published in 1596, contains this passage: The devil, Hate-Virtue, is 'a foul lubber, . . . and looks pale as the visard of the ghost, which cried so miserably at the *Theator,* like an oyster-wife, *Hamlet reuenge.'*

The cumulative evidence is conclusive for the existence of a play on the subject of Hamlet at an earlier date than any at which Shakespeare can have been concerned with it. The general consensus of opinion is that this earlier play was by Thomas Kyd, the author of the *Spanish Tragedie.* Nashe's preface to Greene's *Menaphon,* already alluded to, contains a punning reference to "the Kid in Aesop." Kyd's known plays show marked Senecan influence.[1] The probability that Kyd was the author of the earlier *Hamlet* is further substantiated by resemblances between the *Spanish Tragedie* and Shakespeare's *Hamlet.* In both the motive is revenge; the ghost of the victim relates his story; the hero feigns madness; in each play there is a faithful friend named Horatio; each contains a play within a play; the innocent and guilty alike are involved in the catastrophes.

Although no actual trace of this earlier play has been found, most scholars believe that a German manuscript, dated October 27, 1710, and published in 1781, preserves some material from the original version. This manuscript is possibly a modernized copy of an older one which was

---

[1] He was also the translator of a Seneca-like tragedy entitled *Cornelia,* by the French tragic writer Garnier.

first translated when a troupe of English actors visited Germany at the end of the sixteenth century.[1] The German play is entitled, *Der Bestrafte Brudermord oder: Prinz Hamlet aus Dänemark. (Fratricide Punished, or Prince Hamlet of Denmark.)* It opens with an allegorical prologue which shows unmistakable Senecan influence. Likewise Polonius is here called Corambus, which corresponds with his name 'Corambis' in the First Quarto. For the most part, this German play is exceedingly crude and coarse, although the outline of the plot action follows Shakespeare's closely. It is, however, devoid of literary merit.

To sum up: the story of Hamlet was taken by Belleforest from Saxo's chronicle. Shakespeare received it either from Belleforest, direct, or from an earlier unknown publication of the translation of Belleforest of which the *Hystorie of Hamblet* is a later version, or (as is most likely) he founded his play on an earlier tragedy which was probably by Thomas Kyd. The traces of Senecan influence in Shakespeare's Hamlet are due either to this earlier play or to the general and common influence of Seneca upon Elizabethan tragic playwrights.

[1] The earliest reference known to a performance of *Hamlet* by English actors in Germany is in the year 1626.

APPENDIX B

History of the Play

THE stage history of *Hamlet* is practically that of the English-speaking stage itself. Almost all the great actors of England and America, from Shakespeare's day to this, have appeared as the Prince. In addition, for the past one hundred years, it has been frequently played in the principal European countries. It is safe to say that no other play of Shakespeare's has been more often performed.

Richard Burbage, the leading actor of Shakespeare's company, was undoubtedly the first Hamlet. From the meagre accounts of his style of acting which have survived, we may infer that, like subsequent great interpreters of the part, he was distinguished for the ease and naturalness of his art. The famous lines at the opening of III.ii., 'Speak the speech, I pray you, as I pronounced it to you, trippingly on the tongue,' *etc.* may indeed be a defense of Burbage's style against the more flamboyant method of his great rival, Edward Alleyn.[1] Burbage died three years after Shakespeare and left the rôle of Hamlet for Joseph Taylor, who performed it with applause at the Globe and Blackfriars playhouses until the closing of the theatres in 1642.

After the Restoration, Thomas Betterton achieved great fame in this rôle. He was instructed in his interpretation

---

[1] Because of the different stage conditions and different conception of oratory, all Elizabethan acting would have seemed formalized to us rather than naturalistic. See Alfred Harbage, 'Elizabethan Acting,' PMLA, Sept., 1939.

by Sir William Davenant, who had seen the Blackfriars' company act the play. Betterton for the first time introduced scenery into *Hamlet,* and, if we are to trust the Quarto of 1676, established many of the traditions subsequently followed in acting versions.

David Garrick was the leading interpreter of Hamlet during the middle portion of the eighteenth century. He first appeared in the part on November 16, 1734, and continued to play it many times until he left the stage in 1776. Garrick introduced alterations of his own into the text, one of which was the omission of the chuchyard scene (V. i.), but he was not followed by others in this.[1] The latter years of the eighteenth century saw what many to this day consider must have been the greatest Hamlet of them all, John Philip Kemble, with his sister, Mrs. Siddons, as Ophelia. Kemble restored the text as written by Shakespeare and abolished the Garrick innovations.

The nineteenth century witnessed, in England and America, a number of excellent Hamlets, of whom the best remembered are Edmund Kean, Macready, Samuel Phelps, Fechter, Edwin Booth, Sir Henry Irving, Wilson Barrett, Sir Herbert Tree, Martin Harvey, Sir Johnston Forbes-Robertson, and E. H. Sothern. More recently interpretations by John Barrymore, John Gielgud, and Maurice Evans have made theatrical history. The supposed innovation of 'Hamlet in modern dress' in the late 1920's aroused much controversy till it was recalled that the play was so acted in Shakespeare's time, and even in Garrick's.[2] Ten years later the admirable full-length

[1] See G. W. Stone, 'Garrick's Long Lost Alteration of *Hamlet,*' *PMLA,* Sept., 1934.
[2] See Max Huhner, 'Hamlet in Modern Dress,' *Poet Lore,* 1926.

Hamlet of Margaret Webster and Maurice Evans freshened appreciation and vindicated the staying powers both of the play and the audiences.

Many of the most artistic and remarkable of the modern productions of *Hamlet* have been produced in Russia, where it has had a special vogue, beginning with the novel and historic presentation designed thirty years ago by Gordon Craig for the Art Theatre in Moscow. Nor is there any indication that the popularity of this play upon the stage has dimmed. It still remains the test of the summit of achievement for the art of a tragic actor.

Index of Words Glossed

Figures in full-faced type indicate page-numbers

Index of Words Glossed 217

218 Index of Words Glossed

Shakespeare's First Folio

HELGE KÖKERITZ & CHARLES TYLER PROUTY *Editors*

This facsimile edition, the first since 1910, again makes it possible to own a copy of one of the greatest books ever printed, the First Folio of Shakespeare's plays, issued in 1623. It is now reproduced by modern photographic techniques, and the resultant volume is considerably more convenient and portable than its bulky predecessors. The pages of the new edition measure 8½ x 11 inches, a slight reduction in size from the original, while the text remains legible, a faithful reproduction of the famous Huth copy of the First Folio now owned by the Elizabethan Club at Yale.

Charles Tyler Prouty, professor of English at Yale, has contributed an introduction on the printing of the Folio, the altering of the theatrical texts of the plays, and the playwriting and printing practices of Shakespeare's day.

Helge Kökeritz, professor of English at Yale, has added line and scene numbers so that the Folio can be compared with modern texts. Liberal outside margins and a special paper suitable for writing in ink have been used in this edition to permit annotations. $15.00

Shakespeare's Pronunciation

BY HELGE KÖKERITZ

This comprehensive study of Elizabethan English pronunciation as revealed in the works of William Shakespeare provides a detailed analysis of vowels, diphthongs, unstressed vowels, consonants, and accentuation, and includes phonetic transcriptions of selected passages as spoken in 1600. $7.50

OF RELATED INTEREST

The Composition of Shakespeare's Plays
BY ALBERT FEUILLERAT

Professor Feuillerat attempts to show here precisely what Shakespeare wrote among the plays attributed to him, by analyzing *Titus Andronicus, Henry VI, Richard II, Richard III,* and *Romeo and Juliet*. From a meticulous textual analysis and a lifelong study of the period, he explains many of the mysteries that have long puzzled scholars, demolishes well established myths, and shows the poet at work. $5.00

The Sources of *Much Ado About Nothing*
BY CHARLES TYLER PROUTY

"Undoubtedly he has enabled us the more surely to appreciate the spirit in which the comedy was penned, and any future efforts at interpretation must be tested by reference to his account of the way in which the romantic narratives available to the dramatist have been completely reshaped."—Allardyce Nicoll in the *Shakespeare Quarterly*.

$4.00

The Personality of Shakespeare
BY HAROLD GRIER MCCURDY

Mr. McCurdy sets out, armed with caution and common sense, to discover what a psychological investigation based on the whole body of the plays would reveal of Shakespeare as a man. The results have aroused lively interest and debate among both psychologists and men of letters.

$5.00